P R
FOR

MW00941289

"Never before I. ___ ___ about a generation so relevant and timely. *The Motivated Millennial* will engage, inspire, and empower this generation of leaders. It will help you think differently about your work, your life, and the impact you want to have on the world."

— GREG HEMMINGS, *CEO Hemmings House Pictures and Producer of the award-winning documentary, The Millennial Dream*

"*10 Essentials® for The Motivated Millennial* provides valuable insights from someone who knows how to enter and navigate workplaces to make a profound impact. Whether you are working in a small organization or at a global corporation, Robyn's framework for success will help you guide your career upward. Her advice is grounded in her own proven track record, as well as her insights hiring and promoting top talent all around the world. She knows what high performance looks like, and this book will help you master it."

— JAY FORBES, *Founder, F3 Investments and Past CEO of MTS Allstream, Teranet, and Ingram Europe, Middle East & Africa*

"The world needs leaders now. If you're ambitious, driven, and ready to make a difference in the world, Robyn's advice will help you perform at your best and stand out from the pack."

— GERRY POND, *Chairman and Co-founder of Mariner Partners Inc., award-winning Canadian Innovator and Social Entrepreneur*

"Robyn's advice and insights really help build both confidence and leadership in employees. Her content was a big hit! The positive feedback keeps rolling in!"

"Robyn's *Millennial Mentor* column is a treasure trove of advice for career starters. This book takes it to the next level to help *The Motivated Millennial* who wants to love their work and live their best life."

"Robyn is one of those remarkable, once-in-a-lifetime, inspirational leaders who not only challenges others to perform at their best, but she also creates opportunities and opens doors that allow those around her to shine. She's doing it again in *The Motivated Millennial* where she shares her *10 Essentials*® for career success. A must read!"

"Robyn's advice helps our employees think differently about how they need to guide their careers and contribute to the workplace."

"Robyn oozes empowerment through her relatable and real-life practical experiences. This will leave you motivated, energized, and thoughtful about your own personal and professional life and all that is possible."

— **KELLY LANGILLE**, *Branch Manager, Scotiabank, Saint John, New Brunswick*

"I had worked with Robyn while she was VP of Communications and Public Affairs with our company and always admired her ability to inspire and lead especially in a time of change. The session she just did for us exceeded my expectations. Robyn's material was informative and thought provoking; as she led a discussion with our groups, I know all the attendees learned something new, made a realization, or had an "aha" moment. I know I did."

— **WANDA JOUDREY**, *Director, Bell Residential and Small Business*

"Our team loved it! The information is informative and helped us all expand our knowledge about high-performance leadership, the rise of Millennials, and ways that we can improve our individual contribution to the workplace."

— **JAMIE LATIANO**, *SVP HR, Renovate America, San Diego, California*

ESSENTIALS
for the

MOTIVATED MILLENNIAL

A GUIDE TO HIGH PERFORMANCE FOR
NEW GRADS AND CAREER STARTERS

ROBYN TINGLEY

A book by GlassSKY Inc.
www.GlassSKY.org

10 *Essentials*® trademark pending

ISBN: 978-1-5470-4645-4

Robyn Tingley
www.RobynTingley.com

To my wonderful husband Brent,
and to the miracles of Olivia and Mary Grace.
Thank you for your love and encouragement.

10 ESSENTIALS® FOR THE
MOTIVATED MILLENNIAL

CONTENTS

INTRODUCTION

You're ambitious and motivated. You want to make a difference in the world and feel like you are making an impact. At the same time, you want to enjoy your work, make enough money to live comfortably, and have a lifestyle that lets you stay rested and healthy, with lots of time for family and friends.

The good news is that all of this is possible. It is infinitely possible. But it's not as easy as some might lead you to think. Pop culture makes it look *effortless*. We are bombarded with the Top-30-Under-30 success stories of people who suddenly hit it big. Glossy celebrity culture makes it seem like everything is within reach if we just want it badly enough. Everything is photo-shopped, filtered, and over-the-top fabulous. But mostly, *it's fiction*.

The truth is that living your best life takes effort. It takes focus, *every single day*. First, you'll need knowledge of how to do it, which is where this book comes in. Second, you'll have to do some work. That's where *you* come in.

The fact that you're reading this means you're serious about taking charge of your career and building leadership skills. Congratulations. I'm going to start by saying three things:

1 The *10 Essentials*® are universal.

2 You already have everything you need to cultivate these skills.

3 It's your time.

The *10 Essentials*® are Universal

This book has 10 chapters – one for each of the essential skills you need to cultivate if you want to take charge of your career and your life. The *10 Essentials*® are based on my own journey where I rose up quickly through the ranks of world-class companies and learned from some of the best leaders in the business world. This book is also drawn from the experience I have in hiring and promoting top talent in 25 countries around the globe.

No matter where I have lived or worked, the same defining characteristics kept popping up time and time again. The top performers understood these attributes and mastered the essentials. They applied them consistently and as a result, they always stood apart from their peers. It can take people a lifetime to understand the essentials of managing their career path, and even longer to cultivate the skills. In this book, I've boiled it down so you can hit the ground running early on in your career.

You Already Have Everything You Need to Cultivate These Skills

You have motivation, desire and the ability to focus and apply yourself. You can visualize a better future. You have experiences that have taught you something about yourself – what you can do very well and what you have yet to master. And most of all, *you have time.*

As a new grad or someone who has just recently entered the workforce in the last few years, you have an entire lifetime ahead of you. Cultivating these skills will take patience and practice. You need to give yourself the benefit of time. So many Millennials I speak to feel enormous pressure to have everything figured out immediately. Be good to yourself and be realistic. Life is full of quick wins and slow climbs. My career path was that way and I expect your journey will be no different.

It's Your Time

You are part of a powerhouse generation. While many older colleagues don't necessarily *get you*, you know your worth. You are part of the most well educated, technologically savvy, and globally connected generation ever. You may need to work on your confidence like everyone does when they start out. Unfortunately you will need to deal with your share of unfair stereotypes.

Despite this, you remain socially conscious, ambitious, and chomping at the bit to get your life really started. I understand. I felt that way too. As far as work ethic goes, you have a far better grasp on work-life balance than your older counterparts, and that's a good thing for families, mental wellness and healthcare. It also appears to me that you're not as competitive as previous generations. You value collaboration, true diversity, and team environments. Incredibly, a third of you call yourselves entrepreneurs. These are tremendously exciting assets.

With your sheer numbers, spending power, education levels, and global networks, you are a force to be reckoned with. I believe that when you embrace your full potential and cultivate the right leadership skills, you and your generation are poised to make incredible things happen for societies and economies. You're already doing it. You're on your way. The world is lucky to have you.

To help you get the most value from this book, I've broken it down into general commentary, real life lessons, essential exercises, and a quick summary of key points at the end of each chapter. The more you engage with this content, by learning from the stories and doing the exercises, the quicker you'll soak it up. I wish the best for you as you master the *10 Essentials*® and take your rightful place in this world. After all, it is your time.

CHAPTER 1

MASTER YOUR MINDSET

I'm often asked: What is the single most important step for career success? My answer? Quite simply: *Attitude*.

Attitude is everything. It's the main predictor of success. Not education. Not wealth. Not previous experience. Not even a superior IQ. Your attitude frames every experience you have. It determines how you see yourself, how you set your goals, and how you react to situations and people around you. Attitude permeates everything you do.

And let's be clear here: your *thinking* is where your *attitude* begins to take shape. Since attitude is a product of thinking and it's determined by your ongoing mindset, then you have the power to make your attitude positive or negative. *It's your choice.* It's a choice you need to make again and again, many times every single day because situations are fluid, co-workers change, jobs evolve, and life happens. But when you have a positive attitude, you can deal with what comes up, good, bad, or otherwise.

You might wonder a bit why there is a whole chapter devoted to this topic. It's because it's one of the things that new graduates and career starters struggle with the most. There is a growing body of research that indicates over half of Millennials are at high risk for anxiety and depression. In a survey done by my company, we found that 72% of Millennials surveyed said they do not reflect on what's positive. They are often overwhelmed and struggle daily with seeing the positive aspects in their lives. Only 28% said, "I take time to breathe and positively reflect on all life has to offer me." That's why I wanted to start the book with a serious and timely discussion about how to improve one's attitude, the importance of keeping things in perspective, and staying positive.

You'll find out as we go through the material in this chapter that it takes some level of consistent work and commitment to train your brain to think these ways in the first place, but the good news is that over time, your positive attitude will begin to just happen naturally. Once you recognize that you have room for improvement (*and we all do*), you can actually train yourself to see the positive in all things.

This concept of "training your brain" is an important one to understand. Your brain is similar to other parts of your body in that it needs continuous exercise, but your brain is particularly special. The human brain has the ability to rebuild itself. It's called neuroplasticity. Science tells us that the more we exercise our brain with positive thoughts, the more it will rewire itself to see the positive in situations more easily. In other words, your brain will create shortcuts to find the positive. It's kind of like practicing any kind of game or puzzle. The more you do it, the faster and better you become.

Why You Need to Master Your Mindset

So if this brain training is so great and possible for anyone to do, why doesn't everyone do it? The reason is because overcoming negative mindsets is not easy. Unfortunately negative thoughts can be very powerful and they have a tendency to stay with us longer.

I'm sure you can think of a friend – or perhaps it's you – who constantly replays something negative that happened in childhood. Whenever anyone tells a negative or traumatic story over and over again, to themselves or to others, they risk going into a depression-like state. They've conditioned their mind to fear that event.

Whenever a special date or anniversary comes around, or if they see someone who reminds them of that previous negative event, it can spark difficult memories. Even a song, a movie line, or a casual remark from someone in public can trigger a reminder that causes the event to come flooding back. Since the person has trained their brain to automatically fear that subject, it doesn't take much to break down all over again even though this might be years later. It's like the person *can't move on*.

When someone's mind is stuck in the past, the person will often experience unrelenting negative internal chatter which causes that person to relive past events and harsh negative emotions *too much of the time*. Their brain actually becomes wired to see the negative side of things more often. Over time, these people are more likely to see everyday situations as more challenging and hopeless than other people do. It can appear to other people

7

that this person is living in the past or 'skewed negative'. They get easily frustrated with others and with themselves. You might notice that this kind of person also tends to damage relationships pretty consistently at work and in their personal lives. You'll hear things like 'that person drives me crazy' and they can blow regular events out of control, preoccupying themselves with a trivial matter and wasting other people's time replaying the event.

If this is you or someone close to you, just know that it doesn't have to be this way forever. If you wish to change your mindset, it can be done. And it's actually easier than you think.

Limiting Your Time with Difficult People

We all know negative people like the ones I've been talking about. Personally, I choose to limit my interactions with them. It's not because I don't have empathy for what they experience, but I avoid them because I know that my life is influenced negatively or positively by what and whom I choose to spend my time on.

Instead, I make a habit of choosing to be around people with positive energy and I highly recommend this to anyone who wants to be more successful and bring out their own talents. I choose to spend time with the people who smile and speak encouraging words, the can-do-anything, sky's-the-limit kind of people. I choose to be my best and help others rise to be their best. I believe in abundance for all. I don't have the time or desire to tear myself down and bring others down with me.

Now some people will take great offense and tell you that they're not *negative*, they're just a *realist*. There is an important difference. Positive people can be realists too. They can see risk and identify issues. They can anticipate barriers and appreciate hurdles. They can also be the kind of critical thinkers that we need in workforces. In fact, being wired positively is a huge asset in the workplace.

Why would this be? One key reason is that being positively programmed allows you to see more possibilities and examine more than one side of an issue. Negative people tend to view only the issue at hand and why it won't work and what will go wrong. They stop there. They accept defeat and resign themselves to an outcome they think is inevitable.

But when you pose that same issue or problem to positive people, they'll respond: "What else can we do? Let's brainstorm. We're smart people so let's figure this out." They're happy to explore other ways to get to the best result.

I think you will find that anytime you have positive people around you, you'll see that they are resourceful and believe they can find a way to make things work. They'll pursue success by tapping into relationships to get more information. They are open to learning a new skill, and they may even negotiate a new deadline in order to secure more resources. Basically, they do whatever is needed to work through a challenging situation.

More often than not, positively-oriented people *get it done*. Did they have to try a little harder? Yes. Get creative? Likely. Did they have to put in a few more hours and leverage a few trusted relationships? Probably. But they will succeed. Thus, being in a positive mindset is a huge benefit to any employer. You make yourself much more valuable when you train your brain to see the positive side of things.

REAL LIFE LESSON

POSITIVE ENERGY OPENS DOORS

Imagine that a journalism student in Halifax, Nova Scotia needed to find an internship as part of the requirements for graduation. She was from a small town and always dreamed of working for a magazine in New York or Los Angeles. She particularly loved Ms. Magazine and never missed an issue. Eager and confident, she applied for an internship with Ms. citing her student leadership roles, past writing awards, and good grades.

Two weeks went by without a phone call. Then, a letter came from the magazine. She ran up to her apartment. The envelope was thin, and her heart sank momentarily, but she told herself, "Nothing ventured, nothing gained" as she took a deep breath and opened the letter. *"Thank you for applying to our internship program at Ms. Magazine. We regret to inform you that we do not hire interns who have no professional working experience in the industry. Best wishes as you complete your studies."*

It was short and sweet, and she was out of luck. She felt the sting of the rejection and that could have been it. She could have told herself that she should have known better. No experience. Thousands of miles away. Not even a journalism degree in hand. No established relationships with anyone, anywhere in the magazine industry. *What was she thinking?* She made a fool of herself and should have just understood her limits and settled for an internship back home at the local paper. Unfortunately, now she thought maybe she wasn't even good enough to work *there*. Lots of applicants stop at this point; they become defeated by their own negative thinking.

But that was not *her* attitude. She had no time to dwell on the negative because that wasn't how she was programmed. She was a person who knew about setting goals, reaching for experiences, and being OK with failure. She accepted that it was all just part of the learning process.

Instead, her positive attitude allowed her to quickly consider other possibilities. What about another magazine? She had a few others at her fingertips so she grabbed a copy of Elle Magazine and flipped to the editorial page. She ran her finger down the list of names and numbers, not even sure what half of the titles meant. She found a general number and picked up the phone. She took another deep breath. "Hi, I'm calling from Canada to inquire about student internships with your magazine in New York City. May I speak with someone please who could advise me about your programs?" Before she knew it, she was speaking with a member of the editorial staff who agreed to look at her resume.

"Yes!" she shouted as she hung up the phone and she emailed her resume right away. She got a reply the next day, and she was going to New York. You may have guessed it: *that girl was me*, many years ago when I was a student myself. That experience in Manhattan proved to be pivotal to my early career. Yet it only happened because I didn't let my initial disappointment send me down a negative path. Being positive opened my mind to new possibilities, which in the long term, allowed me to gain new skills and differentiate myself.

I learned a dizzying amount of stuff at the time about the magazine industry, being thrown into it. Plus I got to experience the hustle and bustle of New York City, and I came to appreciate true workplace diversity in a city alive with different cultures and customs. Even better, I was surrounded by strong role models who literally told me every day that *I was good enough*. It was an inspiring place to be as a 21-year-old.

I never forgot the primary lesson in all that and I pass it along all the time. Don't defeat yourself when things might seem bleak; instead train your brain to be positive and use that mindset to find another way to get to the same end. If you hit a brick wall again, keep trying. In the process, you will become ever more resourceful and resilient. These are two tremendously powerful traits that you develop when you live your life from a positive state of mind.

ESSENTIAL EXERCISE

TRAIN YOUR BRAIN

Now it's your turn to try out these ideas for yourself. The more you practice the techniques and ideas we are talking about, the sooner you begin to *train your brain* to respond more positively on a regular basis. This *Essential Exercise* is made up of three easy steps that you repeat a few times to get you thinking in a much more positive way about how to view challenges that arise in your daily life. Let's get started.

1 Begin by thinking about the times when you demonstrated resourcefulness in the face of rejection or adversity, those times when your positive attitude led you to new possibilities. Think about past relationships, jobs, sports teams, grades in school, and financial situations.

2 Write down some notes about what the problem was and what action you took. Then write down the feelings you were experiencing at the time, which could include things like anxiousness, courage, fear, confidence, uncertainty, or whatever.

3 Continue to think about what happened in the end, and make a note of what lessons you learned from that particular experience. By doing this, you'll create positive linkages in your mind and reset past difficulties into positive life lessons.

Now apply each of these steps to four different times in your life where you acted in a way that resolved a problem or issue and you did it with a new or unexpected solution, or overcame some kind of adversity or bad luck.

There are many benefits of this *Essential Exercise*. When you review the times that you were positive, resilient, and resourceful, it reinforces in your mind that you are capable of far more than you might think. Unpleasant things are going to happen at times, but from this exercise, you can see that you have faced challenges before. By practicing these steps and going through this material, you now realize that you have inner strengths, and you have the choice to replace negative thoughts with a much better mindset.

Next time something goes wrong, instead of defaulting in your mind to the worst-case scenario, try to remember how you have already handled other challenges and the times that things ended up turning out OK. Or remember that even though the situation looked awful, you did take away some valuable lessons from what happened. This way you train your brain to see possibilities rather than problems.

You can also start to weave these positive examples from your life into the story you build about yourself and you can use them to illustrate the value you bring to the next workplace or job interview. We're going to talk more about this theme in Chapter 4, when we apply positivity and resilience to the workplace, so stay tuned.

How Attitude Gets You Promoted

Not only will a positive attitude help you see possibilities, which in the long run will allow you to experience more work assignments, gain more skills, and network with more people, it will also help you get promoted.

Employers can hire for skill. They can hire for experience. They can hire for education. But they will *promote* because of *attitude*. They will keep investing in employees who bring a can-do approach to the job and they will give promotions to the people who can constructively solve problems and deliver results.

When you think about it, everyone would just rather be around positive people. It's that simple. Negativity erodes teamwork, it stifles creativity, and it becomes a major drain on productivity. Managers know this. They are not going to promote someone who is always in a bad mood, who complains all the time, and who is forever pointing out all the problems. No great leader was ever praised for making people feel stressed or self-conscious. However you will find that people remember the times they were inspired and encouraged, even if the work was hard.

REAL LIFE LESSON

LOOKING FOR SUNSHINE ON A CLOUDY DAY

Widget-Gadget International had a chance to promote someone to the level of *Head Widget-Gadget Supervisor* for their newest plant. Two internal candidates were up for the job. Let's just call these two people by their attributes and see which one shapes up best.

Let's call Candidate One – Suzanne Sunshine. And for sake of argument, and because he likes to argue, let's call Candidate Two – Oliver Overcast.

Suzanne joined the company three years ago, as a *Junior Line Assistant*, coming in with experience she learned on her last job, which was for a similar style of manufacturer. She has a diploma in General Arts and Science. Last year, she got promoted to *Line Assistant* and started working alongside Oliver. He has now been with the company for almost eight years, and is still in the same role he was hired into, namely *Line Assistant*. Both of them report to the *Head Widget-Gadget Supervisor* but since that person has decided to leave work and return to school, the position has come open.

Suzanne is very good at telling the company story and always speaks positively to others about the value of the products they manufacture. Oliver finds it hard to say anything good about what the company is doing, and he can't be relied upon to speak appropriately to visiting customers or business partners.

In her role as a *Line Assistant*, Suzanne was always ready to support the supervisor when there was a need to gain buy-in from the whole team, especially on key projects and goals. She liked exploring different possibilities and examining all the options and ideas. No matter what kinds of stressful things happened on any given day or what extra work arose, Suzanne kept calm and stepped up to handle the increased responsibilities with the help of her team.

Oliver was quick to point out that he really didn't believe in the way the work was being organized. He was arrogant about it and tended to push only his own agenda in any meeting. He had a habit of putting down anyone else's ideas, and since they seldom reached any kind of consensus, Oliver's team hardly ever got enough buy-in to proceed with new projects. Oliver was quick to blame their lack of success on anyone but himself, and kept insisting that he knew better, if only management would listen to him.

Oliver hit the roof when he was not offered the promotion to *Head Widget-Gadget Supervisor*. He complained loudly that it was a travesty that Suzanne got the nod instead of him. After all, he had been the one working away for eight years, while she had been there only three years, and he kept droning on that he had an advanced degree in Widget-Gadget Technology from the world's best tech institute. It wasn't fair because she only had a useless diploma from the local college.

Was this fair? Why did the company give the promotion to Suzanne rather than Oliver, if he was so highly qualified and had more years of experience? Could it be that no one liked to work with Oliver and that he clearly was not able to motivate or inspire his co-workers? Only seeing the negative side of everything had become an ingrained habit for Oliver and in the end, *attitude* trumped the *advanced degree* as it so often does.

Management will promote *the doers*, the ones who have a good attitude about life and about their abilities. In the end, the company owners knew they could count on Suzanne to work hard and act professionally with anyone she encountered, and that gave her a higher score in her promote-ability ranking.

ESSENTIAL EXERCISE

INCREASE YOUR PROMOTE-ABILITY

So now you understand a little better how managers usually go about building strong teams in a work setting. During my years in corporate life, I have seen that managers consistently tend to promote people who demonstrate specific characteristics, several of which I have listed below. Please note as you read this list over, that each of these characteristics is greatly enhanced when you have a *positive attitude*. Try putting yourself in the position of someone hiring you or considering you for promotion: how would you shape up?

I find a great way to test yourself is to take a pen and think about each aspect mentioned on this checklist. Consider how you would rate yourself in each of these areas in terms of being a beginner, practitioner, or master. Before each one, circle 'B' for beginner, 'P' for practitioner, or 'M' for master. If you're not sure, take this test with a friend you trust and help to rank each other. Often others around us can see in us what we might not.

Your Promote-Ability Checklist

B P M Your ability to positively sell the company story.

B P M Your ability to gain buy-in from the team on key projects and goals.

B P M Your ability to serve as a role model who acts professionally and positively, practicing strong business etiquette and respect for others.

B   P   M   Your ability to see talent in others and inspire them to bring their best to the workplace thus delivering more innovation and productivity.

B   P   M   Your ability to cultivate and maintain healthy relationships with colleagues.

B   P   M   Your openness to explore possibilities and examine all options.

B   P   M   Your desire to learn new skills and challenge yourself with professional growth opportunities.

B   P   M   Your ability to remain calm and focused in the face of stress or increased responsibilities.

B   P   M   Your ability to laugh at yourself when needed and see the humor in life.

Once you complete your ranking, select three skills where you are still a beginner or practitioner that you want to improve upon and take steps to develop more confidence and experience in doing that activity. Ask for help from a co-worker or manager if you need some advice in order to build up your level of skill. Request some more challenging projects to stretch yourself. Take an online course or some training modules if needed.

For the softer skills, become more aware of how your daily routines and reactions at work affect other people around you. Seek out a mentor you respect, someone who is successful in this career path. Watch how they do things. In particular, watch how they relate to their co-workers, the staff who work for them, and to management.

If you realize now that you tend to consistently respond in a negative way, you might consider a life coach, business coach, or counseling. They can guide you to find ways to release any emotional issues you've been dragging around for too long, that are now clouding your judgment and your progress. Surrounding yourself with more positive friends and co-workers is also another easy first step that just about anyone can take to boost their *promote-ability* standing.

ESSENTIAL EXERCISE

INCREASE YOUR POSITIVITY – IT'S AN INSIDE JOB

The key to cultivating a strong positive attitude and all of the rewards it will bring into your life is to recognize that it's an inside job. It all starts within you, in your own head. Every day you must choose – beforehand – how your day is going to unfold. You need to be accountable for the thoughts you think and the words you speak. How you react to situations is completely within your control.

Here are three easy ways that have been proven to rewire the brain over time. Try one technique to begin with. Once you feel success, you'll quite likely be motivated to continue and to also try other new techniques. But for now, just do one at a time, while you build mastery for it.

Set your Intention for a Great Day: When you open your eyes, think about what is going to go well that day and play those things over in your mind. Before you even open your email and consider your to-do list for the day, program your mind positively. Tell yourself that you can handle anything that comes your way. You are smart enough. Resourceful enough. Calm enough. You are going to be just fine. In fact, you'll be great!

Picture the situations you are likely to encounter and visualize yourself smiling, being confident, and being in control. The brain is genius. It will begin to recognize these positive thoughts and intentions, and then it will create shortcuts over time to deliver more positive thoughts to your subconscious automatically. It truly is a brilliant system. When you visualize being positive at the beginning of every day, even in small ways at first, it builds more positivity into your life.

Catch the Invader: Catch yourself at those times when self-doubt creeps in. Begin to recognize what that feels like and what you sound like when it's happening. When that little voice tells you that you don't have enough whatever (money, health, skill, love, patience), *stamp it out*. When you quiet your inner critic, you'll feel better, project more confidence, and attract other positive people into your life. Seek to replace the negative thoughts and self-doubt with more positive statements about yourself: *I am good enough. I am smart enough. I always do my best.*

While you are retraining your mind, accept that no one is perfect so you won't be perfect either. As you are releasing old habits, you might well fall back and react negatively to someone. Old habits are hard to break. But if you do slip up and hurt someone with your words or actions, then apologize to the person you are with. By calling out your own negative behavior, you reinforce to yourself that it's not a desired trait. You also send a strong signal to the other person that you know better and are actively working to stay more positive.

Practice Mindfulness or Meditation: Use meditation each day to contemplate the positive aspects of your life, and visualize your goals. Meditation takes focus and practice, but the benefits are enormous. Increasingly, researchers are demonstrating that people who meditate regularly are able to improve their brains and physically alter them. Over time people who meditate or practice mindfulness become more peaceful and stress free.

Find techniques that work for you, whether it's a morning meditation that you listen to, keeping a gratitude journal, or sipping tea quietly. Use whatever technique you like in order to contemplate the positive parts of your life, while visualizing the next steps and how they'll unfold perfectly for you. Your future self will thank you for it.

The next chapter shows you how to take your more positive frame of mind and create a framework for your life. Everyone can benefit from having a life plan. Having focus and setting goals makes your life simpler and more predictable, and ultimately, more rewarding. Plus when you know where you're going, you're far more likely to reach your destination. I'm so glad you're along for this ride!

- Attitude is everything and you are in full control of your attitude.
- Positive people are more resourceful, see more possibilities, and find ways to drive success.
- Employers invest in and promote people who bring a can-do approach to the job.
- Visualization is like "pre-action" so practice seeing actions and results in your mind first, and imagine them going well.
- Daily meditation is an easy way to program your mind to think more positively.
- When you remain calm and positive, it shows you can handle more responsibility.

CHAPTER 2

CREATE YOUR LIFE PLAN

Successful people have focus. They understand what they want to achieve in life, and they have a plan to accomplish it. Some people call it having vision, some people call it a dream but I like to call it a plan because it's not just about *the what*; it's also about *the how*.

I wrote my first life plan when I was 22 years old. I was hired right out of university by a firm in my local area. My boyfriend (now my husband) had just graduated from engineering school and joined the workforce. We weren't making much money in our entry level positions, and I had some student debt to pay off. We pooled our resources and rented a small apartment in the city a few blocks from where I worked. He spent most of his time and money driving an hour each way to work, but he was employed and gaining experience. Jobs were scarce and we considered ourselves lucky to be working.

Those early days were tight for sure. We had an old Toyota Tercel that we had to jumpstart on cold winter mornings. We re-used and recycled just about everything. I loved to visit thrift shops for new outfits and together we would restore old furniture finds.

We accepted that this was just the start and we were both highly motivated to build a better life. We often let ourselves dream; it didn't cost anything and gave us hope that we'd get it together some day.

One day we were talking about moving out of our apartment and upgrading to something better. We were in a 100-year-old Victorian apartment and there was a bad oil smell in the basement, and that's where our kitchen and bedrooms were located. It was a true starter place. But my husband suggested that we should think hard before moving into another apartment. He thought that we should be paying ourselves instead of paying a landlord.

That was a very nice dream and I immediately pictured a single detached house with a yard. He pictured a duplex in the city with someone else helping us pay our mortgage. That was the first time he told me that he wanted to own apartment buildings. It was a big leap from where we were, and that's when we had our first discussion about goals and built our first life plan.

Our first plan was roughly pieced together but it's interesting when I look back on it that the principles we used that day are the same ones we still use so many years later. In fact, we've used them every New Year's Day when we sit down and write our plan. It's a process that has served us very well over the years. Sharing your goals with your loved ones gives them even more focus, because you can hold each other accountable for staying on track and achieving them.

It was important to me to make this the second chapter in this book and cover this material early in our discussion because 55% of the Millennials who responded to our survey indicated that they wanted to become better at setting and achieving goals, and felt they needed to have the right tools. The process in this chapter is a practical and efficient way to create your own life plan and keep yourself on track while working toward achieving the goals that are most important to you.

What Goes Into a Life Plan

So in essence, a life plan is a set of goals that reflects who you are and what you want to achieve in life, accompanied by a list of actions and timelines within which to achieve that plan. The process of writing a plan is simple enough. You have to think long term and let yourself dream. Don't be constrained by any barriers or boundaries that you might see today. Your plan is not a static thing, but rather it's meant to be dynamic, and it will evolve over time, so don't aim for perfection. As you achieve goals, you'll add more to the list.

And don't be distracted or fooled by what other people might say or think. For example, the plan you create is not intended to be all about a job title you might have written in your high school yearbook, and this plan is not about making a certain amount of money that will eventually make you happy. Keep in mind, money helps you do a lot of things, but it doesn't serve up happiness on a silver platter. Likewise, this kind of life plan won't deliver extreme dreams either such as, "I want to win the lotto and buy a personal jumbo jet."

Instead, what I recommend is that you use the process in this chapter to capture your thoughts. Every idea matters in the creative process. Once you do that, then you prioritize your dreams into what's most important in your life right now – at the time you are building the plan.

Start with the more immediate priorities while still knowing that some of your dreams can come later in life. For now, this process will track both short-term and long-term things so you don't lose sight of those life-long dreams or abandon some dreams prematurely.

The following section outlines the steps in putting your plan together. No time like the present to jump in. What I'm introducing is *The THRIVE Process*. THRIVE is an acronym that will help you easily remember this process and the key elements of your plan, which are Truth, Health & Wellness, Relationships, Investments, Ventures & Adventures, and Education.

ESSENTIAL EXERCISE

CREATE YOUR LIFE PLAN WITH THE THRIVE PROCESS

So now plan a time when you'll be relaxed and free of any deadlines or interruptions. You'll want to set aside a couple of hours for this process. Sometimes the best and most ambitious plans come when you are in one of your favorite places, taking a break, while on vacation or when you've been able to do some meditation. Over the years I've written plans while chilling in a hammock or watching the sun go down. Do what inspires you and have fun with the process.

To get started on your life plan, all you really need is a pen or your laptop, or you can use a whiteboard and marker. You can start this process at any time, and then you will revisit and update the plan at least once a year. When you are starting, it's good to revisit it every three months to adjust where needed or refine goals. Each time you revisit it, you can cross things off that you've achieved, and set new goals for even bigger dreams. Once I got going on this process, I chose to revisit it each New Year's Day because I found it inspiring to set new intentions as I turned the page into a new year. Because it's a long-term life plan, some goals will naturally span several years (like financial goals perhaps) whereas others could take months (like changing your dietary habits).

So begin by writing down the date. You're going to appreciate this years from now when you look back in amazement at what you have accomplished. I love looking back at old plans to see what was important to me at any given time, how much money I was making, and what kind of adventure I wanted in my life at that stage.

Now work through each of the six THRIVE sections below and give yourself enough time to really think and record what you want for these areas of your life.

When you THRIVE, T is for Truth

- **Ask Yourself:** What is your truth? What matters to you most? What do you know to be absolutely true about who you want to become as you go about living your life and growing into your best self? What is your purpose?
- **Set Your Long-Term Goal:** How do you see yourself 40 to 50 years from now? What is the impact you want to have had on others? Is it about social justice? Nurturing? Innovation? Peace? Art? Education? Healthcare? Write down a few lines describing what you want to build toward.

  For example, my earliest plans always listed that I wanted to be an author who helped people in some way, and a philanthropist of sorts, engaging in private endeavors for the public good. I didn't know how I would get there, or what exactly it would look like, but I knew that was part of my longer-term truth – even though at the time I was a new grad and just in my first real job, and had no money left in the bank at the end of the week.
- **Set Your Annual Priorities:** Now that you have focused on your long-term goal, set your annual focus. What will help you move toward living your dream? For example, to take a step closer to becoming an author, I decided to read a book on writing books and getting published. To get closer to being a philanthropist, I decided I needed to get my finances in order to have the freedom to donate my time and money the way I liked, or to pursue social enterprises. This is an example of a multi-year goal that I expected would take me at least 10 years to achieve, but writing it down forced me to think about the actions that I needed to take each year to set me up for future success. You will find more about setting focused actions and creating checklists later in the chapter.

When You THRIVE, H is for Health & Wellness

- *Ask Yourself:* What do you want for your health? Think about your health broadly, and include three things in your thought process: mind, body, and spirit. Are there addictions you need to stop? Are you overindulging in certain areas, yet have a complete void in others? Do you lack confidence or constantly experience negative thought patterns?
- *Set Your Long-Term Goal:* How do you see yourself 40 to 50 years from now? How strong do you want your body to be? How sharp, flexible, and resilient should your mind be? What about your spirit and where you find meaning in your life? Are there patterns in your family you want to avoid or change? Write down how you want to feel as clearly as you can.
- *Set Your Annual Priorities:* Now that you have put some focus on your long-term goal, set your annual focus. What will help you move toward living your dream for optimum health in mind, body, and spirit? What steps can you take now to improve in one or more of these areas?

When you THRIVE, R is for Relationships

- *Ask Yourself:* What are all of the relationships that matter to you? Create a list. For example: I wrote down – I am a friend, daughter, wife, mother, sister, godmother, aunt, volunteer, and mentor. What are you? How often in any given week or month do you need to do something for each of those relationships? For example, you might want to spend more time with your parents than you currently do, but you really don't need to do any volunteering this year. Or perhaps you want to be a better sibling or a more attentive mentor to someone at work.

- **Set Your Long-Term Goal:** How do you see yourself 40 to 50 years from now? How will you have invested in these relationships, and what milestones, reunions, or anniversaries will you have marked? What impact will you have made on people's lives in these key relationships?
- **Set Your Annual Priorities:** Now that you have put some focus on your long-term goal, set your annual focus. What will help you move toward building stronger relationships? Pick two or three areas where you can make an improvement and determine what actions you'll take.

When you THRIVE, I is for Investment

- **Ask Yourself:** How much money do you want? Do you want to have accumulated a certain amount of money by a certain age? What's important to you, and how much do you need to live the lifestyle you want and support the family you might have?
- **Set Your Long-Term Goal:** How do you see yourself 40 or 50 years from now? Are you debt free? Do you own a home? Are you spending your savings travelling the world? Leaving inheritances to children? Setting up scholarships? Opening your own business?
- **Set Your Annual Priorities:** What steps do you need to take now to move toward your goal? For example, in one of my earliest plans, I wrote that I wanted to pay off my home mortgage in five years, and live debt free while saving a certain amount by a certain age. So my annual focus that first year was to meet with a financial planner, set an automated schedule for paying off the mortgage, and put a savings and investment plan in place. I also wanted to get a pay increase. I can trace much of my financial security back to that year and the tangible steps I took.

CREATE YOUR LIFE PLAN

When you THRIVE, V is for Ventures & Adventures

- *Ask Yourself:* What kind of adventures do you want to experience in life? When you were in your early teens, what did you dream about? Did you want to visit the wonders of the world? Climb a mountain? Drive a race car? Snorkel in tropical waters? Volunteer in a developing country?
- *Set Your Long-Term Goal:* Fast forward 40 to 50 years from now. What kinds of adventures have you experienced? Create a list and be as specific as possible. If you want to climb a mountain, which one? If you want to travel the world – to which countries? Make your list long and dream big.
- *Set Your Annual Priorities:* Take a look at your list. Which things can you do immediately, and experience within this year? Adventure doesn't have to be expensive or far away from home. Choose some exciting things that will make you feel alive, but that aren't too complicated. You'll find joy and get the hang of letting yourself pursue these types of dreams. If you can, set up a savings plan just for travel to the first accessible place on your list, and know that each month, you are contributing to your dreams.

When you THRIVE, E is for Education

- *Ask Yourself:* What do you want to learn? Do you want to complete more formal education? Certifications? Do you want to learn to play an instrument? Do you want to read the classics? What about a foreign language?
- *Set Your Long-Term Goal:* Fast forward 40 to 50 years from now. Write a list of all that you have learned. Big and small. Formal and informal learning. Include the skills you mastered and where those skills have taken you.

• **Set Your Annual Priorities:** What steps do you need to take now to move toward your goal? For example, if you have always dreamed of going to college or university, set a goal to research schools and save some money for tuition. If you've always wanted to learn a new language, set a goal to watch more TV in that language or listen to some online learning modules before investing in a formal program.

When you THRIVE, You Turn Your Plan into Action

By now, you should have a very robust plan with macro long-term goals that are based on key areas of your life, supported by annual priorities that will move you forward. The next step is to get out a calendar and think about tangible targets and activities that will support your annual priorities. Schedule the actions realistically. Ask yourself what steps you are going to take each week, each month, or each quarter to build toward success.

I find that it is very useful to break your plan down into "Weekly To-Do Steps" so you can stay on track. The smaller the steps you can implement, the greater the likelihood that you will stay committed and succeed. As you achieve these smaller goals, you will be motivated to do more and you'll find that sustaining your focus becomes easier.

REAL LIFE LESSON

PERSISTENCE PAYS OFF

When I teach the *10 Essentials®* and *The THRIVE Process*, people ask me if there is an area of my life that I found particularly challenging ... a skill that was hard for me to cultivate, and I always tell them about my struggle with *work-life balance*.

I consider myself a very healthy person, with a high energy level and an intense *joie de vie, a joy for life*. My drive for success is strong and I've always felt pretty much invincible. Early on in my career, I would regularly pull all-nighters and be able to go for days without sleep. I would crash on the weekend. My diet was coffee, soda, salted anything, and fast-food burgers just about every day. The word *exercise* was not even in my vocabulary.

Even so, I knew it was good to have goals about my health, so each year I would set targets in my annual plan about how much weight I would lose, how often I would work out, and all the healthy recipes I would try to cook at home. I consistently failed to reach any of these goals. I never lost weight, never managed to get to the gym consistently, and I didn't like to cook, so why bother? There were so many better things to do with my time and I always had excuses. In truth, none of these things mattered enough to me, so they weren't authentic goals.

This approach went on for years. I would set health goals and toss them aside. Coaches at work would tell me to relax, take time to look out the window, or go to a spa. I thought they were crazy. Didn't they know I was busy? *Didn't they know they were paying me to work?*

But what they were seeing, that I had yet to register fully, was that I was having some lower back pain. They could see me moving uncomfortably in my chair, crunching pain killers, and sometimes even bringing a heating pad to work with me to dull the sensation. I just got on with my day. I was highly functioning despite everything and I was busy working on other goals, so my philosophy was that I'd just deal with the pain. It never occurred to me that my body was trying to send me a signal.

I would have driven myself into the ground I suppose, but one day my doctor said that he thought we should do an exploratory day surgery to see if there was something present that the scans and tests weren't picking up. Two hours after going under, he woke me to tell me that he'd removed a significant growth related to my reproductive organs and he diagnosed me with endometriosis.

He said there was no cure and women just live with it. The tissue grows, builds up, starts to get uncomfortable, and they can continue to get surgeries as needed or take prescriptions. The drugs he recommended for me would be regular monthly injections and by the way he said casually, my fertility was likely already compromised. *Huh?* I was in my late 20s and this was a major wake-up call.

It got real, really quickly. Up until then, my work-life balance goals had no substance at all, but suddenly that changed because now I had a real goal. I had to find a way to heal myself and defy the odds of not being able to get pregnant. I wanted children so I read everything I could about hormones in food, preservatives, aspartame, sugar and so on.

The first two years I tackled food. I taught myself how to eat and fuel my body in the correct way. I gave up beer and soda cold turkey and I still don't drink those. The next few years were all about self-care, meditation and exercise. I joined a gym and spent time with a trainer. I even worked with energy healers, acupuncturists, and therapists of all kinds.

The good news was that I found myself in the best shape of my life and had been pain free for years. As far as I was concerned, I was healed. So why wasn't I getting pregnant? I went to see a naturopath and a fertility specialist. Never in a million years could I have imagined myself in those offices, but there I was. I kept the dream alive that someday I'd have children.

But even with all of the hard work I'd done to transform my life, they said even the very best technology in the world would only give me an 8% chance of conceiving. The endometriosis had damaged my ovaries, one fallopian tube was blocked, and of course, I was then past my prime child-bearing years.

As bad as this sounded, I refused to give up. I asked how other people had beaten those odds. They mentioned vitamins but didn't hold out much hope for those. They also said that some patients found yoga helpful. It wasn't exactly what I was expecting, but it was something. So I broke all that down into little goals and milestones, things I knew I could do so I wouldn't become overwhelmed and give up.

I spent six months purposefully *slowing down*. I went to see a naturopath, did daily yoga, and went to a masseuse for the first time in my life. I immersed myself into the world of herbs, vitamins and breathing. I maintained my exercise regime and my healthy hormone-free diet. I got blood work done regularly, and when we saw an improvement, I went for it. And now, we have two lovely children who are the best treasures we know in life.

The lesson here is that it took years for me to come to grips with my health, and even when I finally woke up, it took tremendous effort, education and commitment to stick to it. But it was all worth it in the end. Now my goal is about maintenance. With all of the information that I possess, there is no reason for me ever to fall back on bad habits.

Explaining the Mystery of Continuing to Thrive

Overall in my life, it has been fascinating to me how well *The THRIVE Process* has worked in helping me create the life I want. I still review my plans several times a year, but really, because I have internalized this process for so many years now, and I've learned to set goals the right way, I find that just making the plan is what delivers the success, as if by magic, *all by itself.*

It's gotten to the point that if I say something is going to happen, I inevitably orchestrate things to make it happen. It's as if once I set the coordinates, my mental GPS gets me there. If I set a goal to launch a company, land a client, or heal a part of my body, it happens. *I get there.*

But surely, you might be thinking, there has to be some actual material reason for all this magic? Things don't happen out of thin air. I have asked myself this too and I really thought about *why*. Why is it that writing down my personal and professional goals and plans works so incredibly well? When I meditated on this, six key reasons appeared and I'm happy to share them with you, so you can truly understand the magnificence of this system and apply it to your own life.

1 *Set SMART Goals.* I ensure that my goals are SMART ones, and I have become very adept at breaking down my big dreams into SMART goals, ones that are specific, measurable, attainable, relevant, and time-bound. I will talk more about how to set SMART goals in Chapter 10 when we talk about work-life balance and dig into time management.

2 *Ask for Help.* I have become very good at asking for help. If I realize I don't know something, I don't hesitate to ask for help. I reach out to people who know about things that I don't. I tell them what I'm looking for and I ask them to teach me. In the last few years, I've opened an online retail store, built my own website, learned about the publishing industry, and launched my own company – all with the help of fantastic advisors.

3 *Speak Your Dreams Out Loud.* I share my dreams. This sounds like such a simple thing but a lot of people are afraid to tell others about their dreams. They're afraid to be judged. Afraid of public failure. Afraid they'll jinx their chances of success. But here's the thing. Sharing your dreams will actually *increase* your odds of fulfilling them. It truly works. I tell people I trust what I'm trying to accomplish and it's beautiful in three ways: their support motivates me further; their advice guides me in helpful ways; and the very fact that they know about my goals holds me accountable to achieve them.

4 *Be Future Focused.* I find that I have become future focused. I don't dwell on the past. If something goes wrong, I learn from it and move on. Tomorrow is another day. I know I'll do better. Life is too short to beat myself up over mistakes, so I just take the lesson and move on.

5 *Visualize Success.* I have discovered and harnessed the power of visualization. This is still a little bit magical too, but it is a concrete action that really helps in manifesting what I want. The truth is that you can write the fanciest, most comprehensive, and practical plan there can be, but if you don't believe you can actually achieve the goals in your plan, *then you won't*. You have to believe you can achieve the goals you set, and you have to feel them before they've arrived. I've done a lot of reading about techniques for manifesting and the law of attraction, and I have become a strong believer in the power of the mind. Your thoughts create things, so make your thoughts the right ones!

6 *Celebrate Your Wins.* I have been successful in achieving my life plans because I celebrate my wins and I am truly grateful for them. I believe there is more than enough to go around for everyone and that we can all succeed in becoming healthy, wealthy, and fulfilled. Therefore, operating from this place of abundance for all, I express gratitude and celebrate my wins every day. I say thank you when I wake up and again every night when we dine as a family.

This is a tradition that I am teaching my children. Gratitude shapes your attitude in a profound way. I also keep journals where I log all of the wonderful experiences in my life. I have journals that date back for years. I rarely read them, but every now and then when we move houses or I'm cleaning out closets, I'll discover an old one and read through my dreams and accomplishments from that time period, and it reinforces to me that I can achieve whatever I set my mind to.

Unlocking the Magic

These are the reasons I can point to as to why *The THRIVE Process* is so powerful. Now it runs itself as I have explained, but in the early days, when I was still building confidence and competence, I kept my written plan very close at all times. For years, it was a standard beside my bed and I looked at it several times every week, just to stay focused.

If I was falling behind in some area, I took lipstick and wrote that point on the bathroom mirror, reminding myself every single morning and night about that specific goal. Sometimes it would stay there for months until I reached a point where I could move on to something else. Use whatever techniques you feel will work for you, and just see what does the trick for you in your life. You can unlock the magic the way I did, and once you gain confidence in yourself and the process, the sky is the limit.

The key is to just do it. Don't just read about it, but sit down and commit your ideas to concrete plans and goals. Become focused on what matters to you and what you want to achieve in life. Set your priorities, break them down into smaller goals, and tackle them in sequence. You will be amazed at what you can achieve!

ESSENTIAL EXERCISE

REVISIT AND UPDATE YOUR LIFE PLAN

Imagine it's New Year's Day. You're entering a new year and are looking forward to setting some goals and resolutions for the coming 12 months. Before even thinking of what you want to achieve, pull out your plan for the year that has just gone by. Hopefully you revisited it each quarter, so you have good notes, some check marks, and maybe some revised dates. You could also have some things that you didn't quite get to yet. Or if it's your first time through this process, then congratulate yourself for getting started and jump in. Here are the six steps to follow.

| *Celebrate the past year.* Grab a bottle of wine, your favorite snack, and cozy up by the fire with your closest friend. Make sure to have your gratitude journal nearby, that's where you write down what you are thankful for each day. Talk about your year's highlights. Think about all the wonderful things you did. Use your past plan or last year's agenda as a guide to jog your memory, but also add some things that weren't on your plan. Go through your social media feeds and smile as you relive all the wonderful parts of your life and the things you experienced in the last 12 months.

Now make a special note of these things:
- Did you go anywhere special – near or far? Where?
- Did you meet any new people? Who?
- Did you celebrate any family milestones?
- What about new foods, new music, or new hobbies?

I love looking back at my gratitude notes too. I like to include something funny someone said, place names, or even what the flowers smelled like on a certain day. It's a wonderful way to keep a diary for yourself or for your children for the years ahead.

2 *Think about how much you've grown.* Write down any new skills you learned. Think about what you learned about yourself this past year and list at least three things. What did you release this past year that was no longer serving you? This could be relationships, bad habits, negative thoughts, or a go-nowhere job that had run its course. Make a list of the activities that boosted your confidence and gave you more self-assurance, and again, try to list at least three things.

3 *Express gratitude.* Who do you want to thank? New Year's is a great time to send notes of gratitude to people and lift them up as they enter a new phase. It can be just a quick note like: "Hey there. I was just going through some old memories from this past year and wanted to say how much I appreciated it when you did *x or y.*" It will make you both smile. Write up and send at least five of these notes.

4 *Turn to your Life Plan.* Reflect on your life plan from the previous year. What did you accomplish? You can use a spotlight technique of "green/yellow/red" to indicate what you accomplished (green); what you worked on (yellow); or what you didn't complete (red). Now think about what you want to carry forward. Are there some goals that must continue into the next year, some that you didn't quite manage to tackle, or some that you no longer need?

5 *Apply The THRIVE Process.* After you've captured all you've done and the lessons from the last year, think about what's next on your list. Use *The THRIVE Process* to capture your goals for the coming year. First write down the "carry forwards" and then consider and add the following:

• Do you have any dreams you haven't written down yet?
• Did your process this year reveal new opportunities you'd like to experience?
• Is there anything you've been afraid to write down that you want to stretch yourself to reach this year?

6 *Share and hold yourself accountable.* Pick a few of your top goals and share them with people you trust. Ask them to help you stick to your plan by offering moral support, checking in with you regularly, and gently reminding you if they see you getting off track or engaging in behaviors that don't support your bigger goals.

The next chapter dives into the importance of being self-aware. When you understand your natural strengths and build on them, there is no limit to what goals you can achieve. Self-awareness can supercharge your life plan and give you a true competitive edge in fulfilling your life's goals and helping others perform at their best.

KEY POINTS FROM CHAPTER 2

- Successful people have a clear focus and solid plans that help them sustain momentum and achieve goals.
- Use *The THRIVE Process* to guide your goal setting.
- Break down your plan into annual goals, monthly milestones, and "Weekly To-Do Steps" so you can stay on track.
- Make time to celebrate your wins and be grateful because this will keep you motivated.
- Review your annual goals and key milestones at least every four months and make adjustments if needed.
- Revisit your life plan at least once a year to update it and continue to stretch.

CHAPTER 3

KNOW YOURSELF
AND BUILD FROM THERE

Did you ever meet someone with such a strange personality you wondered, *What planet are they from?* Or maybe on occasion you have asked yourself, *Why do I seem so completely different sometimes in comparison to my friends?* Any time you put people together at work or in any kind of group setting, the various personality quirks can cause havoc. Then again, if you can create the right mix of personalities, it can become a truly productive team dynamic.

In fact, I believe that once you start to think about personalities in a newer and fresher light, you'll understand better how we all bring different mindsets into the workforce. The world of work is not just about the money we earn, but it's also about finding a balance with regard to our overall internal value systems, and finding what works with our unique personality. Taken all together, the knowledge I'm going to share in this chapter can really help you discover your purpose in this world.

While our drive to find a purpose-driven career path is admirable, it's easier said than done. The day-to-day realities of student debt, monthly cell phone payments, and starting families inevitably creep into the equation.

But don't sweat it if you don't exactly know what your calling is. *Most people don't*, especially those just starting out.

The truth is that you don't just wake up one day and say, "Aha! I know that *this* is the reason for my existence and *this* is where I'm going to focus all of my energy." It would be awesome, but life is just not that simple. Most people have to *work* at finding their purpose in life. But when they do, the payoff is worth it. I believe that when you become clear on what you are driven to achieve, you'll be able to reach your boldest professional and personal goals.

This chapter is devoted to ways to become more self-aware, to clearly identify your strengths, and to incorporate feedback along the way, starting with personality indicators. The knowledge that I gained from personality measurement tools was a complete game changer for me, and I've seen it work with virtually all the other people I've worked with. It's time to make it work for you and this chapter will show you how.

The Science of Personality

When you understand how personality works, it takes the mystery out of personal interactions and this will be a huge success factor in all parts of your life. Let me briefly explain where these personality indicators came from and why they are so influential.

Since the dawn of time, people have been trying to figure out what makes each other tick. In Ancient Greece, Hippocrates studied what he called the four moods of people, and his theory was down to earth, actually based on the natural elements of fire, air, water, and earth. Plato went on to describe four personality temperaments in his own way, calling them philosopher, guardian, artisan, and scientist.

It was this early work that laid the foundation for what we know as modern personality assessments. These are basically questionnaires that are designed to reveal the true characteristics of the individual. The most frequently used tests in the marketplace today are: the Myers-Briggs Type Indicator, DISC, and the Big Five Factor Test.

But let's consider how these modern tests developed into what you see today. Not much actually happened in the field after Hippocrates and Plato. It was not really until the early 1900s when Sigmund Freud started talking about the power of the mind. His theories had an unprecedented impact on this field of thought, and took the idea of personality traits into a more modern understanding.

When Freud was doing his work, a variety of theories and tests emerged within the broader field, which allowed us to peek inside the personalities of ourselves and others. Those tests ranged from analyzing aspects of handwriting to questionnaires that tried to gauge emotional evenness for recruits in the US army.

But perhaps the greatest impact on personality testing came in 1921 when one of Freud's earlier colleagues, Swiss psychiatrist Carl Jung wrote the book *Personality Type*. He was the first to propose that people always prefer certain behaviors if they are given free choice and that these behaviors can be categorized into different personality types.

Once it was accepted that personalities could be measured and categorized in a practical way, another classic tool was developed that is still in use today. First popularized in 1942, it's called the Myers-Briggs Type Indicator (MBTI), and it's still taken by millions of people each year all around the world. The MBTI method was based on Carl Jung's theories and was further refined over the decades by Isabel Briggs Myers and her mother, Katharine Cook Briggs. It offers a simple test and interpretation to help people quickly and easily understand their personality type.

A few years after the MBTI method was first suggested, a Harvard psychologist named William Moulton Marston created the DISC system to explain the emotions and behaviors of people. This system was used in the US Army's recruitment process and then later become popular in the business world. About a decade later came another tool called the *16PF* and then a popular test called The Big Five Factor test, which proposes that all behaviors can be categorized into five adjectives. Each of these popular tools can be quite insightful when you want to figure out what makes you tick.

Real Life Lesson

How Self-awareness Pays Off

When I became more self aware and learned how to collaborate in the best way with others, it changed the whole trajectory of my life. I was only in my early 20s, when the employer at my first real job out of university invested in Myers-Briggs training for me and the team I was on. The results that I took from that first workshop were something I've gone back to time and time again throughout my career because I learned about my natural tendencies, my organizational style, how to avoid pitfalls, and just a whole pile of useful things.

Once I figured out the fundamentals about how I operate, I knew why I like things a certain way, why I get along with certain types of people, and why I find certain tasks easier than others. I also learned how to collaborate with other people who see things differently than me, and how to tell an introvert from an extrovert. Every other person you meet has their strengths and ways of doing things and once I realized how to recognize the patterns, *it was like gold to me.*

You know why? Suddenly, I could tell if someone on my team needed more detail or more time to process information. I figured out ways to structure deadlines and work flow to make sure our jobs got done on time, even if I needed to depend on others who saw the world (and the problem) *completely differently* than I did. It was as if I had gained a new language to use when

I operated in groups. I learned to show that I truly respected differences and wanted to collaborate with others in a constructive way, and did it ever make my work life easier.

When I dug into my own results on that personality indicator, I was also able to gain the confidence to build on my own strengths and excel in the areas I was naturally already good at. This let me avoid detours on my career path into areas that wouldn't have made me happy anyway.

I can't even imagine what my career would have been like without this base, which is why once I got the chance to lead my own work teams, I invested in personality assessment tools for each team member. I wanted them to learn about themselves, each other, and the team's overall personality. That way if we needed a better balance of personalities, we knew exactly which type of person to look for the next time we did a hire, so that we maintained a good productive mix of different perspectives and approaches. I frequently went back to those assessment results, particularly if we had a conflict emerge or if we missed a deadline, or when we needed to get more innovative as a group.

ESSENTIAL EXERCISE

GETTING PERSONAL – IT'S ABOUT YOU

If you've already done one of these personality test indicators before, dust it off and read your results again. Because you've grown since you last did one, you'll no doubt rediscover some points that you can use right now. If you've never done a test like this before, take 20 minutes and do one online. It's easy to do. Just search for 'Free Personality Test' on the internet and you can complete your own assessment.

In doing so, you'll get some background analysis and a customized report that highlights your strengths and weaknesses. You might find a list of 'preferred' and 'non-preferred' behaviors, which is what some tests call it. Seek out a test that provides practical tips on how to deal with colleagues, friends, and family members given your unique personality profile.

If you can attend a longer workshop, that's really great. You might also ask your HR department, since they likely have a personality assessment process they recommend. Once they find out that you're interested, they may even approach your team and offer it to the whole group. If they do, then everyone can benefit from the insights these assessment tools offer and your team dynamics have the chance to really improve exponentially.

Many of the online sites offer tips regarding your career path, so if you're not sure you're in the right workplace, a test like this can help you decide on what type of career you are better suited for. Your personality profile will tell you where you would be happiest and best able to make the highest level of contribution.

Among other questions, you'll find out things like:
- Do you like interacting with people? Or do you work better on your own in a quiet space?
- Do you like detail or are you a big picture thinker?
- Do you prefer a clean desk with everything neatly in its place or do you operate better with piles of paper around that you can see?

The answers to these questions and more will help unlock a lot about your personality strengths and the type of environment you will thrive in.

Bringing Out Your Best

When you know your personality type, you become more aware of your strengths and weaknesses. Some people think it's possible for individuals to cultivate each characteristic equally, but if this is possible, I've not seen it done very often. Most of us stick to what we know and what we do well because it's naturally what we're good at. And likewise, we shy away from areas that cause us stress and where we fear we might fail.

If you're like me, you may receive lots of well-meaning advice from managers and mentors in life who will tell you *to focus* on your weaknesses. I have heard that too, where I was told to go to work in areas that I wasn't good at so I could get a taste for it and learn those skills. But personally, I think that's the wrong advice. It's a distraction that will take you off your path.

Here's the way I see it. We're here to be our best and bring out our best. The way you are going to shine in the workplace is by focusing on what you're already good at. That's not to say you should avoid areas you don't know anything about. That's not what I'm saying. But you shouldn't seek to make your weaknesses your bread and butter. You might develop a way to be good at it, but your heart won't be in it and you won't be able to fully excel the way you could if you were to focus on building upon your natural strengths.

Another reason to take your personality type seriously is that when you know yourself and what causes you stress, you can see it coming and manage it more effectively. Too many people find themselves stressed out and ask: *How did I find myself here?* They have no idea what set them off. But when you know what you are sensitive to, and you know how you respond to criticism, authority, and change, it gives you the knowledge to manage yourself and your interactions better. I think you will find that your greater level of self-awareness will go a long way to avoiding sleepless nights, and feelings of inadequacy or frustration. You'll begin to proceed in life with much more confidence, poise, and competence even in the heat of a situation.

REAL LIFE LESSON

PLAYING TO YOUR NATURAL STRENGTHS

I remember when I was Director of Communications and wanted a promotion to the job of Vice President. I had been performing well and some of the senior executives took notice. They thought since I was doing well in public relations and media, that I would do equally well in Investor Relations.

When they asked me to take a parallel move into Investor Relations, I was flattered but a little conflicted. In a way I thought, wow, that would be great, such a big challenge. I knew it was a vote of confidence, and it could be an excellent way to expand my skill set by learning about that new field where I would be more exposed to finance, and have regular contact with the analysts. I didn't want to say no and disappoint anyone, and I thought if I didn't take it, I might send the wrong signal that I wasn't ambitious enough or I didn't want growth.

But the inner conflict was still there. Because I was really clear on my strengths, I knew in my heart that this move was not a good fit for me. It was one thing to get exposure to this area, that would be a positive move for my career path, but it was quite another thing to lead the team, becoming *the face* of it with the financial analysts and experts, and to direct a team who had much deeper knowledge than I did in that area.

Given what I knew about myself, I could see nothing but stress, a huge learning curve, a credibility gap, and frankly a whole lot of time stuck behind a computer working on spreadsheets and in meetings with financial types. Nothing about that excited me in the least.

It was a tough decision, but I passed on the move. I didn't know what the full repercussions would be to my career, but I felt strongly that I needed to stick to what I was naturally good at and what made my heart soar. I was making a fantastic contribution where I was and there were still things I wanted to accomplish within Communications.

I did however take the lesson away that the senior executives wanted me to learn more about other areas. I immediately took an increased interest in finances. I found a coach on the Investor Relations team who helped me improve my skills at deciphering financial numbers and become more proficient in that area of the business. She was generous with her time and very patient with a creative type like me. In turn, I helped her present her ideas and communicate the numbers. We made a good team, and both improved as a result of our partnership.

I also dove deep into my own area's finances and became much more adept at predicting costs and valuing the investments we were making. And I took leadership training, which was really far more up my alley. I loved it. I was glad I didn't have to lead in a completely different part of the company that I just didn't have any major interest in.

Overall, I was much happier as I continued to learn and grow in my own role. One year later I found that my perseverance and hard work paid off. I was appointed as Vice President of Communications and I was the youngest person ever in the company to reach that position. I believe that I was able to excel and earn that promotion because I was true to myself and knew myself well enough not to get distracted by other shiny opportunities that just didn't fit my personality traits and natural strengths. At the same time, I invested the extra effort to gain new skills and show that I wanted to grow and deliver the best results I could within my area of strength.

How to Build Stronger Groups and Teams

Along the way when I was working in corporate, one thing I learned a lot about was managing conflict. It's only natural that conflicts are going to surface in the workplace since it can be a competitive environment at times. Since there are limited resources, anyone can face stressful demands on their time and energy. Let's face it, you won't always get along with everyone. If you are aware of the various personality types, you will be able to anticipate not only what sets you off – but also what sets others off – and in that way, you can prepare accordingly and minimize the damage.

Besides that, diversity is a positive thing on teams, so make it work to your advantage. I have seen cases where *group think* became a real concern in the workplace, where some teams had too many people who thought in very similar ways. While it's good to have lots of strength in key skills within certain departments – you may want a lot of nit-pickers in audit for example – personality assessments can help identify gaps on the team. Groups that intentionally strive to be more inclusive of different types of personalities can make better overall decisions and offer more well-rounded ideas.

Personality assessments are also great when you might be getting ready to pitch to a big customer, enter into a new partnership, or if you need to persuade senior management to make a major investment in your area. Chances are that the person across from you at the negotiating table has a different personality style than you, so you'll have a strong advantage if you know some of the ways to interact with that different personality type. You'll also be aware of your own very strong tendencies and it will serve you well to realize when it is a good idea to park your strengths briefly in a meeting or to flex them, depending on who you're dealing with.

Very often, when sophisticated teams have a very important pitch to make and they really know everyone's personality, they can make highly strategic decisions about the order of the speakers, who will speak to which topics, how long each person is given in the meeting, and so on. When they build the agenda for the meeting on the insights they have about their own team members and the preferences that they know exist in their audience, it's an excellent set up for success. I have found that the end results for that kind of meeting are always better because of the time and thought that went into planning it upfront, taking all the personality types into consideration.

So now you know that having a personality assessment done is very valuable and highly recommended. But once it is done, you still need to be open to feedback from those around you in order to keep learning and growing. You'll still be offered input on a daily basis by peers, team members, and your bosses about how you're doing in your interactions. Most people will avoid this because it can be uncomfortable, but I encourage you to cultivate the skill of taking feedback and doing it gracefully.

Listen carefully to the input from your manager, and make it a point to solicit feedback from other colleagues too. So after a meeting, you might ask what you could have done better. Also ask what was particularly useful. You don't have to create a big survey or make it formal because sometimes that makes the other party uncomfortable, but do make a point of soliciting input. It's how you'll grow stronger. And then tell your manager that you've done so because you're committed to continuous improvement. They'll applaud you for it and your maturity will be evident.

ESSENTIAL EXERCISE

FIGURE OUT WHAT TRULY INSPIRES YOU

Once you start to know yourself better, you can think about your passion and calling with more clarity. In addition to being in tune with your personality type, I have found that the following techniques are excellent ways to get to know yourself better and tune into what is truly in your heart. When you do what you love, your workday becomes so much better and time passes quickly because you are bringing your best skills and talents to the table. Try the following four steps to see where your heart is leading you next.

Let yourself dream. By the time most people enter the workforce, they've supressed some dreams, and maybe even forgotten how to let themselves dream. They have become preoccupied by their daily responsibilities and routines. To overcome this and get back in touch with your inner self, find a quiet space and set a timer for one minute. Write down all the things you believe you are driven to achieve in life. Do you want to bring water to billions who don't have it? Write a best-seller? Inspire people through art? Become a philanthropist? Be an amazing parent?

2 *Know your zone.* Take another minute for each of the following three questions. I suggest 60 seconds because that encourages you to use your gut instinct with no second guessing or judgments. 1) What do you value in life? 2) What are you so good at that you could teach it? 3) When do you lose track of time? Now look for similarities between your dreams and the answers to these questions.

3 *Reality check it.* Take your list and share it with parents, teachers, and colleagues. Ask them to help you identify jobs that support your interests. This process is key to making sure you are fully exploring your options. These people know you best and can help you brainstorm about jobs that you might not even know exist or suggest new relationships you'd do well to develop.

4 *Take action.* It's up to you. Nothing takes the place of action. You need to try a few things and gain hands-on experience to know if you are on the right track. Don't get caught up in finding the perfect job that makes you happy every day. It doesn't exist. Life is full of challenges and you'll need to improvise, but these few steps can help you lay the groundwork to ensure your compass is pointed in the right direction.

The next chapter is all about taking what makes you unique and building a personal brand. When you proactively manage your reputation and know how to promote your skills, in the right way and with the right people, you'll be able to open more doors and be even more successful.

KEY POINTS FROM CHAPTER 3

- Take a formal personality assessment test and use it to your best advantage.
- Clearly identify your natural strengths and build on them, then be ready to flex them when needed.
- Encourage your workplace to provide personality assessment tools to your team or work group, and use what you learn collectively to build capacity.
- Pay attention to peer reviews and feedback as a way to highlight your strengths and identify growth points within your daily work.
- Be open to team diversity and make it work for you.

CHAPTER 4

MANAGE YOUR REPUTATION

It has always been true but today, even more than ever, *Branding means business*. This relates to you because you are in the business of managing your own personal brand. Everyone needs to *proactively manage their reputation*. Are you currently doing a good job of it or do you need some practical tips to boost your brand?

If so, you're in the right place. This chapter explains how to identify the elements of your personal brand and effectively create your unique story so you can present it to the world. Plus I'm going to explain how you can leverage social media and avoid reputation pitfalls.

The good news is that you're already sitting in the corner office when it comes to *your personal brand* and you are fully in charge of your public image. You are your Chief Reputation Officer. It's your job to make the best impression possible at all times, 24/7. This task requires constant diligence and is full of pitfalls if you're not proactive – especially in today's world of social media where your reputation is vulnerable at every second. But it doesn't need to be a daunting process. Cultivating your personal brand just takes a little upfront work and some regular maintenance.

Controling the First Impression You Make

Let's think about: *How can you best market yourself to potential employers or clients?* A good place to start is with your first impression because if you don't make it over that hurdle, you'll likely end up out in the cold.

Psychologists have spent years trying to figure out how long it takes for an individual to make a first impression. The average time is seven seconds, that's all you've got to get off on the right foot with a new colleague, manager, client, or potential business partner. In just those few moments, the other person makes a judgment about you: *Are you safe? Dangerous? Friendly? Approachable?*

And importantly, it doesn't have to do only with *what you say*, you are also judged through non-verbal cues. In fact we as human beings have been hardwired to judge each other from the time we started interacting with each other, going all the way back to our days in caves when life depended on the survival of the fittest. Today, your challenge is to be aware of this reality, and use it to your best advantage.

Becoming good at creating a positive first impression is critically important if you want to strengthen your personal brand. You can make a huge impact just by offering a warm, genuine smile with strong eye contact, and a solid handshake. And don't underestimate the value of good manners, tidy hair, and selecting clothes that are a match to what you want to achieve or accomplish.

Once you look the part and feel confident, pay close attention to your body language, as well as the other non-verbal cues that you are projecting. Ask yourself, what is your body language conveying? Think seriously about your posture, your smile, your eye contact, and your handshake. Are you standing up straight with shoulders back and head up? Is your smile warm, genuine, and engaging? Are your eyes open and bright which tells people you see them and acknowledge them?

This next point might seem a bit old school but it's not: *you need to know how to shake hands properly*. Whether you like it or not, a solid handshake show respects and professionalism, setting the tone for your meeting while creating an immediate perception of your abilities in the mind of the person you are meeting. A handshake that is barely there won't do, and there's no need to pull the other person's arm out of the socket.

The sweet spot for a handshake greeting is in the middle. You want to show confidence with a firm handshake – one hand firmly and pleasantly grasping the other person's hand for just a few seconds. There's no need to touch someone's body any-where else. You've only just met and you want to be respectful. Different cultures will warrant different greetings, so be mindful of the people you are meeting with and ask about proper etiquette beforehand if you know you will be meeting with people from other countries or cultures.

The other non-verbal cues you send are just as important such as what clothes you're wearing, your hair, your make-up, and your accessories. I also suggest you think about your technology. What are you looking to demonstrate? Sophistication, status, flare, and creativity? What about just being clean and organized? Think about the culture of the workplace or the setting of your meeting: is it relaxed, formal, or somewhere in between? What clothes would be appropriate to your role? What kind of personality traits might be assumed because of how you are dressed?

REAL LIFE LESSON

MAKING AN IMPRESSIVE FIRST IMPRESSION

The job had not even been officially posted but the company didn't need to spend time advertising. They already had several hundred resumes that came in online when they had hired for a similar position several months before. When they called the top potential candidates from the existing list of names, they were in a hurry and gave the individuals less than 24 hours before the interviews were taking place. *No time to waste.*

When Juliana got the call, she was working at her retail job and was thrilled to be considered. She told everyone in the store that she would soon be moving on, and proceeded to spend the evening texting friends and posting potential job outfits and accessories on social media to solicit her friend's opinions about what she should wear.

A barista named Daniel was also happy to get a call out of the blue from the company; he had applied the previous summer and had sort of forgotten about it when a different person was hired at that time. But he still really wanted to break into the field so he switched his shift that was on the next day and started to prep what he needed for the interview.

The next day, the HR manager set up the small boardroom at 8:15 a.m. and was only giving each person 30 minutes or less. He knew what he was looking for and since it was an entry level job that they filled several times a year, he was determined to narrow the field that morning to the top two people.

Daniel was up first, walking in wearing a sharp business casual look, his cell phone was turned off and in his pocket, and he had spent the previous evening making some notes about questions he wanted to ask. He brought a paper copy of his resume and his references, just in case they were needed and those were tucked in a simple black notebook along with a pen. Daniel placed the notebook down immediately on the table upon entering and stayed standing while he shook the hand of the HR manager. He met his gaze during the greeting.

They both sat down and the interview proceeded positively from there. Exactly 25 minutes later, the HR manager wrapped it up and stood up, so Daniel stood up too. He expressed a sincere thank you, shook hands once again with the HR manager to say goodbye, and gracefully exited the boardroom and the foyer. He felt pretty good but was a bit nervous as he walked past four hopeful faces on his way out. He smiled and thought, *Well, I did the best I could.*

Juliana was seated nervously with the group of candidates still assembled. She was tired because she was too restless to sleep the night before, still unsure of her outfit. She had hundreds of suggestions from well-meaning friends and was still scrolling through their comments the next morning from the moment she woke up.

She had let herself get distracted, and as a result, she didn't allow enough time to pull herself together in a professional way, let alone prepare her mind. She still appeared disorganized plus she had her head down focused on her phone when her name was called. She jumped up and hustled into the small boardroom.

She realized at the last minute that she didn't bring any paper but fortunately, there were some blank pages on the table. Instead of shaking hands, she immediately sat down and started rummaging through her purse for a pen. But when she found one, it didn't write. She thought no problem, I'll take notes on my phone. The phone was her constant companion but it looked messy, as it always did because she never wiped it down.

Juliana felt she was able to answer the questions quite well once she settled down, but each time she felt she should take a note about the expectations, salary, and reporting structure, it was distracting because she had to turn her phone back on and tap away, but that meant she didn't keep eye contact very well with the HR person. Twenty minutes later the interviewer stood up to signal the meeting was over, but Juliana thought she should still ask a few more questions so she would appear super keen about the job.

Unfortunately, it became awkward because the HR manager was determined to move through his schedule and she wouldn't stop talking. He finally ended up walking her out of the room through the foyer to the elevators and he pushed the down button. Once the elevator arrived, she entered and waved goodbye nervously. As the doors closed, she let out a huge sigh of relief, glad that the nerve-racking meeting was over.

The next day, Daniel and one other young women got a call for a second interview while Juliana got an email that said thank you but we have decided to go with another candidate. The lesson here is to think about the impression you want to make and really prepare for that.

Pay attention to all the details of your appearance, your demeanor, and your technology. Ask a mentor you trust for some advice on what to wear and what to say. It's a good idea to do a mock interview so you can practice. In particular, practice entering the room, shaking hands, and being seated until the process comes naturally. Run through some sample questions they might ask you, plus some specific questions you might ask them. Then practice saying a sincere thank you, shaking hands once more, and exiting the meeting room in a professional way. Whether it is a client, a job interviewer, or a potential business connection, you want to make a solid impression so they know you feel confident about yourself and your abilities.

Identifying Your Personal Brand

It's not just in meetings and interviews that you want to exude confidence, but every time you are in public. Practice ways to impress upon people the best aspects about yourself and your background without being boastful and while you are at, express a sincere interest in them too. When you engage with others, meet their gaze, and speak face-to-face, you'll gain more confidence each time.

As you travel through life, it's important to take some time to think about the way you want others to perceive you. Are you reliable? Funny? Hard working? Well educated? High energy? Uber-responsible? A financial wizard?

Once you decide how you wish to be seen, then use that to cultivate your personal brand. You need to know yourself well, and be selective about which parts of your story and your background you want to emphasize. It can be tempting to put everything you've ever done in a single profile, or share your entire list of life accomplishments in one interview. But the reality is that when you provide too many details, you can dilute your story instead of strengthening it.

When employers are searching your name and scanning literally hundreds of resumes, you need to stand apart from the pack. The following *Essential Exercise* gives you some ideas of how to help you get crisp and be very selective about what you want to highlight when you talk about yourself and have a chance to sell your qualities to someone else.

❖

ESSENTIAL EXERCISE

CREATE YOUR BRAND MESSAGES AND PERSONAL STORY

Start by choosing five to seven characteristics that most align with your personal self. These will form the basis for your own brand. In other words, what do you want to be known for?

If you are stuck, try this. Create a list of all the jobs you've had, including summer work, internships, or volunteer roles you took on, basically anything that offered you an opportunity to build a new skill. Then write down all the skills you learned and the characteristics you developed from those experiences. Maybe you never missed a shift as a lifeguard or a server, so you not only learned those skills, but you can also say you are reliable and hard-working. If you were a cashier, you likely gained customer service skills and you know how to process payment transactions of all kinds.

Now think about where you added value in each of your past jobs or opportunities, and turn that into a skill. Maybe you did a volunteer project with some friends and you took on all the social media promotions for the event. Those are skills you gained. If you have not had the chance to be in the workplace or do much volunteer work then think about school projects or assignments that you particularly enjoyed and any extra-curricular activities where you learned new skills.

Now ask yourself what others would say about you. Would your best friend agree that you embody the skills and characteristics that arose above? What about your colleagues? Your family? Ask them to give you some feedback about how you are coming across.

Just a quick caution here. *Not all feedback is created equal.* Your friends might know you as a dog lover, but unless you are working at the SPCA, this is not likely going to be one of the top traits you want in your personal brand in terms of career advancement. You might also have a wicked sense of humor and pull the best pranks in the world, but again that isn't something you would necessarily want to play up.

The next step in creating your brand is to think about times that you exhibited the positive personal characteristics and skills that are most important. Give at least two examples for each brand characteristics. Now, think about photos you have that show you behaving this way and any recognition you've received for doing these things. You can use these images on your web profiles to reinforce your brand.

Now you have a pretty solid list of brand attributes you're happy with so write down two to three sentences that summarize these things, bringing out the best aspects of yourself. An example could be, "I am a goal oriented problem-solver who loves to deliver on time, every time." Or "I am a creative writer and accomplished communicator who's been published online and in print."

Write a few more crisp sentences to describe your approach to work and you can use these when responding to questions or in your online profiles. These basically become your elevator pitch, which is a 30-second personal statement that you can say whenever anyone new asks you about yourself.

The final step is to weave it all together, combining your personal characteristics with your strongest skills into a one or two minute concise summary. Practice telling your chronological story about where you've been and where you want to go in the most compelling and succinct way that you can. Getting your personal story down to just a few minutes will take some effort, but will serve you well. You will be so much better prepared for networking events, interviews, and ice breakers where you have to meet new colleagues.

ESSENTIAL EXERCISE

PROMOTE YOUR STORY

Having a good brand to promote is just one part of effectively managing your reputation. Reputation is defined as what others think of you. You need to create moments to share your story and cultivate an understanding of what makes you so unique: *Why should people trust you, hire you, or promote you?* Below are the top ways I know that you can put your best attributes to use as you proceed to set up and advance throughout your career.

- **References do matter.** Employers still use references regularly to validate their selections, sometimes even checking them before an interview. You need to anticipate this and have a strategy. A common mistake people make is to simply ask (or worse yet, *text*) contacts for a reference. But I suggest that you don't leave this to chance. If you expect someone to endorse you, tell them the type of job you are applying for and what skills it will require. Jog their memory with examples of the work you did so they can speak well of you, and so they can give thoughtful input into the process. They are an extension of your image, and you need to manage this part of the process as carefully as you manage everything else.

- **Create a biography.** In today's world of mergers, reorganizations, and virtual workers, sometimes our managers and teammates change very quickly. Often, we don't even have the opportunity to meet them face-to-face before we need to deliver on big projects. My advice here is to create a one-page biography about yourself, and send it along proactively to any new bosses, important colleagues, or potential clients. Include a short note with your bio that says something like: "I thought you might like to learn a little more about me and how I can contribute to the company. You'll see I have experience in *x and y*. I would appreciate the opportunity to discuss this further with you when the time is right."

- **Keep your social media clean.** These days it's common practice to look someone up on the web to find out about their work background and their interests. Sweep your social media accounts, LinkedIn profile, and resume to clean up anything that erodes your personal image or doesn't reflect well on your brand. Check your privacy settings to make sure you are deliberate about what is private for friends and what is public. Create new pages if you need to by making your own website, Facebook page, blog, or YouTube channel, whatever is relevant to the work you want to do, and that will add credibility and give you a positive profile.

- **Be consistent at work.** On the job, it's important to cultivate your brand daily, especially with the colleagues you see all the time. Many people get too familiar with colleagues and reserve their 'game face' only for the boss. That is a costly mistake. Your reputation is something you build over time through consistent behaviors. I advise that you remain friendly but professional with colleagues at all levels and at all times, because that is what will get you a promotion or a referral for a special project.

- *Manage yourself well.* Remember that the world of work is a group sport. Being an effective team member is critical to maintaining your reputation in the workplace. Do you talk too much? Do you invade people's space? Are you disorganized and miss deadlines, which ultimately compromises the team? If you need to do better, remember that self-awareness is a powerful tool. We've already spoken about personality assessments in Chapter 3 and I suggest that you use them to better understand your natural tendencies and where you may need to flex your personality to show more or less restraint, expression, organization, or the like. The few minutes you invest in taking a personality assessment will help you reflect on your personal style in an objective way, and show you how to make any course corrections when that may be needed.

- *Pay attention to sneezers.* I use the word *sneezer* to describe enthusiastic early adopters of new ideas. They are the people who have their finger on the pulse of the organization and others look to them for their opinions on what is new and what's the next big trend. A *sneezer* is a very good person to have on your side, because if they like you and believe in you, they can become one of your best cheerleaders, spreading the message quickly about you or your good work. A *sneezer* is someone with the power to talk you up in a positive way to others in the group, and you should seek to find ways to help them as well, so that it becomes a mutually beneficial relationship. Just be aware that *sneezers* can be found at any level in the business, from entry level or assistant to a vice president or director, so you need to be nice and get along with everyone, in order to discover these people and cultivate solid connections with them.

The next chapter shows you how to keep your personal brand current and competitive. Continuous learning is a must in today's work environment. You'll learn how to create an inventory of your skills and build a learning plan that will keep you sharp in the face of constant change.

KEY POINTS FROM CHAPTER 4

- People form an impression of you in seven seconds so make those moments count.
- You own your personal brand and it is your daily job to cultivate, promote, and protect your image.
- Be aware of how people perceive you and strive to always make a good impression.
- Pay attention to your skills, education, presentation style, handshake, and what you wear.
- Impress upon people the best parts of you and your background without boasting.
- Sweep your social media accounts, resume, LinkedIn profile, and speech patterns to present a positive impression to anyone who looks up your name or meets you.
- Know your own story and find moments where you can share it in the best way with others around you.
- Cultivate strategic relationships with the *sneezers* within your organization because they have the potential to talk up your qualifications and abilities to others in the group.

CHAPTER 5

CONTINUE TO LEARN AND GROW

Our world today changes at a rapid pace. No one can guess what type of new technologies or regulations will emerge in the coming years and how they will forever change the way we all work together. But there is one thing for certain: change will always be with us and we all need to be flexible.

How will you prepare for inevitable change? How will you stay competitive when your job or your industry changes? It's absolutely imperative that you keep your skills current and marketable if you want to continue to advance.

Most people get some kind of formal education or training and then call it a day. That approach used to be fine when very little changed at work. It wasn't that long ago that people worked in the same company for decades with the same people, doing work that stayed relatively the same week after week, year after year. But as you well know, those days are gone. In today's world, the continuous learner is the one who will thrive.

Continuous learning is the constant expansion of your skills. It is the ability to view all of your experiences as potential learning opportunities. Continuous learners are extremely valuable to employers because they are willing to reexamine their assumptions, methods, and practices.

ESSENTIAL EXERCISE

CREATE A UNIQUE SKILLS INVENTORY AND LEARNING PLAN

There are five steps in the process of continuous learning and an important component of this process is determining what you need to learn. We'll begin this process with Step One where you'll learn to understand the difference between soft skills and hard skills. Then in Step Two, you'll learn to create an inventory of the skills you possess in each category, soft and hard. In Step Three, you'll put your ambitions down and think about what skills you are missing between what you know and what you still need to learn. In Step Four, you'll build your learning plan and in Step Five, it's all about practice.

Step One: Understanding Soft Skills and Hard Skills

Both soft skills and hard skills are important, but most management experts agree that while hard, technical skills will get you the job, it is your level of and proficiency in soft skills that will help you keep that job and get you a promotion. Soft skills are sometimes described as social skills. They include your ability to interact with people and relate to others. Your soft skills will help you, or challenge you, in your interactions with colleagues.

Soft skills are based on your personality and tendencies, but they can be improved upon through practice, if you know what areas you need to work on. Often volunteer work provides wonderful opportunities to practice soft skills and become more proficient in social interactions. It's all about how you relate to people and operate within your work environment.

The other set of skills are hard skills and they include technical expertise. They are ones you have been taught. Hard skills can be measured like math or programming capabilities, or possessing a foreign language. Typically, hard skills require some kind of certification, and the fact that you possess these skills can usually be tested and quantified by some kind of external body or standardized test.

Step Two: Create a Full Skills Inventory

Now it's time to create a full inventory of skills you possess in each category: soft skills and hard skills. Think back to Chapter 4 when you were creating your brand identity and you were thinking about what skills you possess. That's a good jumping off point for this exercise.

To help you think through this, I've provided a list below of some common soft and hard skills. As you reflect on these, consider if you possess any of these and think of any others not listed. The goal is to create a substantial list for yourself. This will help you in so many ways including beefing up your online profiles, articulating what differentiates you, flagging any transferable skills that could apply to new roles, and of course, building your confidence. Through this process, you will begin to appreciate just how much you do know, and how qualified you currently are.

Examples of Soft Skills

- Strong Work Ethic – hard working, willing to work, motivated, loyal, takes initiative, on time for work, regular attendance at work.
- Positive Attitude – happy, pleasant, enthusiastic, bright, optimistic, cheerful, encouraging, confident, willingness to be flexible.
- Good Communication Skills – articulate, responsive, good at listening, oral, written, speaking and presentation skills.
- Negotiating – persuasiveness, empathy, ability to 'replay' what you heard, listening, having a win-win mindset, open minded.
- Leadership Skills – motivating, inspiring, can create the vision, can clearly sell the vision, can build effective teams, deliver results, good at navigating change.
- Time Management Abilities – organized, scheduled, effective, on time, respectful of calendars, realistic in allotting time for work, attention to detail.
- Problem-Solving Skills – creative, can bring people together, open to new ideas, willing to explore different angles of a situation, decision-making skills.
- Acting as a Team Player – agreeable, supportive, self-aware, cooperative, active contributor, knowing how to flex by leaning in or pulling back when needed, willingness to learn.
- Self-Confidence – self-aware, positive, clear on your focus and contribution.
- Emotional Evenness – calm, cool-headedness, objective, diplomatic.
- Ability to Accept and Learn From Criticism – adaptability, ability to reflect on oneself, objectivity, perspective, willingness to learn, appetite to grow.
- Critical Observation – strategic thinking, connecting the dots, understanding existing relationships and influences, lateral and vertical thinking.

- Conflict Resolution – being able to see all sides of an issue, finding common ground, listening, understanding trade-offs, finding what people value most.
- Responsible – hold yourself accountable, reliable, self-disciplined, conscientious, common sense approach, resourceful.
- Courtesy – manners, etiquette, business etiquette, gracious, says please and thank you, respectful, culturally sensitive.
- Flexibility – adaptability, willing to change, life-long learner, accepts new things, adjusts, teachable.
- Integrity – honest, ethical, high moral standards, does what's right even when no one is watching.
- Interpersonal skills – nice, personable, sense of humor, friendly, nurturing, empathetic, has self-control, patient, sociability, warmth, social skills.
- Professionalism – poised, clean and well-dressed, projecting that you 'have it together', neat appearance, well spoken and knowing not to use slang or profanity.
- Customer Service – courtesy, pleasant, ability to get repeat customers, ability to win back customers, empathy, listening.

Examples of Hard Skills
- Knowledge of Machines – operating machines, fixing machines, different methods and standard operating procedures for machines.
- Software Development – specific creative skills, technical language skills.
- Foreign Language Skills – ability to communicate at some level in another language, comprehension, conversational, written.
- Project Management Skills – methodologies, risk management tools, software.
- Change Management Skills – knowledge and experience with specific methodologies.

- Basic Computer Skills – Windows, MS Word, Excel, PowerPoint, Outlook, Google Applications, MAC.
- Data Analysis – how to collect and analyze data and trends, present data for any purpose.
- Math Skills – good with numbers, calculations, accuracy.
- Specific skills or knowledge of tools in any of the following fields – finance, accounting, audit, tax, legal, ethics, risk management, IT, construction, manufacturing, logistics, medicine, archeology, oceanography, geography, tourism, trades, import, export, marketing, or sales.
- Certifications in any field or trade – learned a body of knowledge, tested by an authority, earned credentials by that authority.

Step Three: Closing Your Skills Gap

In this step, you are going to identify new skills you want to learn that will help you to get to the next stage in your career or advance your personal ambitions.

Start by thinking about the job you want to have in the next three to five years. Next, do some research to find out exactly what skills a person in this job must possess. You can find job descriptions online through a simple search. Find recruitment web pages and LinkedIn sites that post jobs. Review these in detail and be realistic about which skills you possess and identify any gaps.

If the job you want is in the company you are currently working for, take a look at the competencies identified for the role you want. You can find these in a job description posted on the company's internal career site or job board, or through a chat with the HR representative or a manager. Sit down with your HR representative because they can guide you and help you round out the skills that you need to include in your plan, both in the short term and longer term. Just the act of sharing with HR that you have a plan, and that you want to grow within the company can very often set you ahead of other colleagues.

Here's an example. If you are looking to advance into people management or farther up in your organization, ask to see a copy of the leadership competencies and develop an understanding of what this looks like within your workplace. Often, leadership competencies will include things like business acumen, financial understanding, people management, and selling the vision. Again, you might inquire of the HR department what specific steps you can take over the next years to prepare yourself for a leadership position.

Then outline the ways you are going to gain each skill. Are you going to ask to shadow someone for a few months? Maybe you could read a book that HR recommends, attend training, or raise your hand to volunteer for a project that you know will give you more exposure to these types of jobs. Set a specific goal in your annual plan about how you are going to develop the new skill or skills that you need. The next step below will help you to do this.

Step Four: Build Your Learning Plan

Identify the ways you are going to gain the skills you need. There are a variety of ways to learn new skills. Pick a realistic number of skills you want to gain and set deadlines for learning each element. You may have to break some of them down into smaller steps and master each requirement in sequence.

- **Books or Magazines.** Trade magazines within specific industries often describe different jobs or give ideas of specialized courses you might consider taking online or in person.

- **Free Webinars Online.** Seek out reputable webinars or courses that offer a proven deliverable and a measureable result, such as a certificate of some kind. Be cautious because very often a free online webinar is just a sales pitch to get you excited to sign up and pay for an elaborate and usually expensive training package or coaching situation offered by an "expert". Some of these have value but you have to do your homework to ensure that what is being offered is legitimate.

- **YouTube Videos and Podcasts.** There are all kinds of training videos by experts that you can access free online. Some will be more relevant and helpful than others.

- **Classes or Resources Offered by your Employer.** Many companies have libraries of resources or specific in-house training programs that you can access to build your skills or enhance your knowledge of the company processes or the context within the overall industry.

- **Conferences and Trade Shows.** Regional, national, and international industry gatherings almost always have learning components built in to the schedule, so you can seek out a two or three-day conference where you can take specific modules of learning and obtain credit for completing them. There are also very valuable networking opportunities that are built into major conferences and you may well find that connecting with a larger peer group can really open your eyes to what is out there for you in the future within your career path.

- *Classes at Community College, University, or Technical Schools.* Traditional in-class learning and distance learning options are available to just about everyone, in a wide range of career paths. Find out what courses are highly respected within your industry and be sure to meet with your HR representative to see if your employer will pay for part or all of your tuition. If it is out of your own pocket, it may still be worth the investment.

- *Engage a Teacher or Tutor.* This may be a better option if your learning does not match up with a given course or existing program. Seek references from the individual to make sure you are a match and that the teacher or tutor does have the knowledge or ability to help you achieve your specific goals.

- *On-the-Job Learning.* This is by far the least expensive and most effective way to learn because you are getting paid while learning and you don't have to give up your free time. Ask your HR representative if you can participate in specific learning in your own part of the company and within related areas of the company. When you can cross-train, you become even more valuable to your employer and other areas of advancement become open to you.

- *Job Shadowing.* This is another very effective way to learn new skills because you tag along with an existing employee, usually someone with a high level of knowledge and expertise, and you get to learn what their job is all about. Treat this as if you were in school by taking notes and asking questions, in order to get the most from the experience.

- *Travel with Your Job.* When you travel to other divisions or countries within your career path, you learn a tremendous range of new information, plus you become immersed in different cultural contexts, new business environments, innovative approaches to work, and different languages. Sometimes you may learn quite specific skills. Take any and all of these opportunities that you can because it very often rounds out your overall career education and awareness in a significant way.

- *Join a Special Interest Group.* Seek out and join a social group at the local library to learn a new language, a new computer skill, or other common interest that adds to your skill sets. Check your local listings for free classes that are offered on a variety of topics. You might even find and join a volunteer group in your community that is planning to do some development work abroad. Joining a group like that can open you up to highly valuable connections, skills, and life experiences.

Step Five: Practice, Practice, Practice and Stay Alert!

Being a continuous learner takes constant practice. You need to be open at all times and inquisitive so that you can tune into potential new opportunities whenever something is mentioned at work or in the community, or when you see something online or on TV. Not all opportunities are obvious so keep your eyes and ears open.

Here are some techniques that I find are excellent ways to make the best of all potential learning options out there. Practice these things frequently, until they become like second-nature, and you will always be ahead of the pack.

- Ask questions when you don't understand something.
- Take notes to increase your chances of retaining the information.
- Ask for feedback and advice from more experienced co-workers and learn by observing respected colleagues or practitioners whenever you can.
- Watch for trends and new processes in your industry and try to get in on the ground floor of any new training opportunities.
- Ask to become part of a special project at work that you know will be a stretch for you.
- Develop your own learning goals at work and in your personal life because you are the best expert on yourself.
- Recognize your preferred learning style (such as learning by seeing, hearing or doing) and try to select courses and teachers that offer the kind of learning that works best for you.
- Apply the lessons you have learned from past experiences to new situations.
- Become more open to trying new ways of doing things.
- Maintain your new skills by practicing what you have learned as soon as you can.

Who Do You Need in Your Corner?

In addition to identifying the skills you need to develop in order to progress in your career, it's a great idea to seek out different types of people to guide and help you, that match with what you need. I like to think of there being three important types of teachers you can choose to learn from and they are called mentors, coaches, and sponsors.

Often the terms *mentor* and *coach* get used interchangeably. I tend to use the following definitions for clarity as a way to distinguish how each type of person can benefit you in your career. After the definitions, I'll give you some techniques that will help you find and work with each kind of person.

A mentor is someone who gets to know you and who works with you on general goals. A mentor may be assigned to you formally through a mentorship program at your organization, or you may seek out a mentor in your industry because you realize you need one. A mentor starts by getting to know you fairly well, paying attention to your current path, and understanding the goals you have set for yourself.

A mentor will typically have more experience and expertise than you and often more seniority. They don't necessarily have to work in the exact same company or field as you, and you would seldom have a direct reporting line to your mentor. In fact, I have often seen it be more helpful if your mentor is an arm's length away from your day job. That way, they can be objective and not get caught up in internal work priorities or specific personalities.

When you find the right mentor, he or she can help you round out your thinking as you contemplate various options such as career moves, skills you want to gain, and networks you want to access. Ultimately, their role is to provide advice as you consider your overall career goals. A mentor can also help if you encounter roadblocks or need a door opened.

It's a good idea to revisit a mentorship relationship every six months to make sure that it's still effective. If you think that it might be time to move on, be gracious in thanking them for their help and the time they have given you. I find at this point, if you ask a mentor if they might still be willing to chat or consult occasionally in the future, they will say *of course*, which is a great feeling. This way you leave things with them on a positive note.

Now, let me define and talk about what I mean by finding and working with a coach in a career sense. Please note, I am not suggesting a *life coach* here, but rather someone to help you through a specific skill, goal, or situation that you are facing. In this case, look for someone who has done the job before so they can help you learn the ropes. A coach in this context fully understands the duties of the job you are doing and the complexities of the situation you are handling, so they are ideal to walk you through what needs to be done.

So for example, here is one way a coach can be extremely valuable. Perhaps you are a risk taker and high achiever and as such, you naturally find yourself in a situation that you have not been in before. You've just accepted a stretch assignment and been given the responsibility for something new but you need to hit the ground running. You just don't have the luxury of learning at a slow pace because the stakes are high.

This is an ideal time to find a coach who can give you training, guidance, or specific advice to help you navigate your new role and fulfill the duties effectively and efficiently. The time you need that coach for will be determined by the situation. It might be for two weeks, a few months, or even up to a year, depending on how challenging your work environment is, how complex the processes are, and what level of leadership role you might be tackling.

I used a coach once to help me through a labor dispute because I had never encountered one before. I only needed the person for the duration of the dispute and we did a debrief together afterward which was also really helpful. I sought out a coach because I specifically needed to know how to process the heavy flow of information I was receiving from many different sources who all seemed to have their own agenda. There were also political minefields and strong personalities to manage. The whole thing was time sensitive and I had to build my capability quickly and efficiently so hiring a coach was the perfect solution.

Now, let's turn to the role of a sponsor. A sponsor is an individual who is in your organization. Sponsors operate at the most senior levels and have influence over things like promotion decisions and who gets selected for high-profile training programs. They act like your personal champion, endorsing you for key roles and special projects. They give you significant profile with the senior executives, help you network with the right contacts, and strategically open doors for you. It's a good idea to get a sponsor if you want to achieve a significant role in your organization or have your employer invest in your career or education in some tangible way. Later on in the chapter I'll give you some tips on how to find a sponsor.

REAL LIFE LESSON

WORKING WITH A COACH

Joe was recently given a really big challenge at work, something that he had been hoping for but he knew it would be a steep learning curve. The company owner had put him in charge of all the aspects of a new installation of technical equipment within his department. The process was complicated to work out, it had to be completed within budget, and there was a tight timeframe. As a Production Supervisor, Joe had assisted with installs before, but now it was all on him and he felt the pressure. It was a stretch assignment for sure.

Before agreeing to it, Joe asked his mentor if he thought Joe was ready to take on something like this, and his mentor said yes, but advised Joe that it might be a good idea to find a coach to help him with the internal logistical issues since there was no room for error. Joe agreed and he asked his HR representative for a recommendation of someone who could assist him.

HR said that there was an employee named Pete in another division who was an expert in installation of new technology so he introduced Joe to Pete. The two men arranged to meet once for a two-hour strategic planning meeting and they discussed the most important parts of the task, focusing on what to watch out for and working out the testing protocols at each step which were a critical element of the installation process.

Then Pete agreed to be on-call to Joe for one-on-one consulting if Joe needed any further help, if questions arose, or if specific trouble-shooting was required. Pete was a valuable coach to Joe on the project and after the six-week mark, when all the testing was proven and the project was complete, Joe and Pete met once again in person to celebrate a job well done.

REAL LIFE LESSON

FINDING A SPONSOR

This story is about Hugh who determined that he could benefit from securing a relationship with a sponsor from inside his company, someone who was above him in the organizational chart. At first, he thought maybe he should look for a mentor, but then a colleague explained things to him this way: a *mentor* helps with general goals, a *coach* helps with specific goals or skills, and a *sponsor* is a person who can help an employee achieve a specific job or reach a desired level within the company they both work for. Yes, Hugh thought, a sponsor was exactly what he needed.

At the time, Hugh was working in a global organization as a Director of Sales. He was based in the United States, and his work took him to many different cities across the country. He dreamed of someday having a senior executive job that would report directly to the CEO. Currently, he reported to a vice president.

He had many peers at the same level in the organization who were equally ambitious. He decided to make his interests clear to his manager and ask for support.

He knew the company conducted an annual training program for strong performers, and that it was a bit of a training ground for vice president roles. He wanted to have that training, and he knew that through that program, he would get exposure to senior executives, to the CEO, and that he would have a chance to demonstrate his talents. There was a rigorous application and selection process for 10 coveted spots, and the process involved getting an active endorsement from his manager.

Hugh scheduled a meeting and conveyed the following to his boss. Hugh said he was very interested in advancing. Some day he wanted to work globally and at an executive level. Hugh admitted he had a lot to learn, but he was ready. He shared his accomplishments and skills, using the elevator pitch he had developed. He shared that he had thought of some ways that he could learn from his boss and from others about how to make an even stronger contribution to the company.

Then Hugh asked his boss if he would consider the following points. Hugh asked if they could meet each week to discuss his work deliverables. Hugh said that he admired the manager's style and wanted to pick his brain about how he had developed his own executive skills. Hugh specifically asked that if a global project surfaced, would the boss consider putting Hugh on it so he could gain the knowledge of what it's like to operate across different countries and cultures?

Hugh added the fact that he had been researching the executive training program and would like the manager to go to bat for him and endorse his application, because having his sponsorship would carry a lot of weight. Hugh assured him that he would put together the rationale himself, that he would shine in the interview, and that he would deliver on the exercises in the program.

With this logical and specific request, Hugh won over his boss and secured him as a sponsor to help Hugh get into the training program. Once in the program, his boss remained in his corner. Hugh knew that this would be a stepping stone to securing even greater sponsorship for future promotions.

ESSENTIAL EXERCISE

SEEK OUT YOUR OWN MENTOR, COACH OR SPONSOR

To Find a Mentor:
- Look around for someone you admire. Does this person seem accessible to you and open to a conversation?
- Think about what precisely you want their help with. Get clear on your request. Would you like this person to give you direction, provide a sounding board, or help you understand how to build out your life or learning plans? Be specific with how much time you would like them to spend with you, how frequently, and if it would be in person, or by phone or online.

- Reach out and ask for a call or an appointment. Be clear about the reason you want the meeting. No sense wasting your time or theirs if they don't have time for any mentees at this point.
- When you secure the meeting, prepare your pitch: what exactly are you hoping to learn, how can they help you open doors, and do you expect them to see opportunities for you or introduce you to specific networks or whatever.
- Follow up immediately afterward with a thank you, and some proof of action that you've taken based on their guidance.
- Be on time and prepared for all subsequent meetings and review the commitment each six months.

To Find a Coach:

- Think about a skill you need to learn in order to do your job. It might be to operate a machine, navigate software that you don't understand, or build a website when have no idea where to start.
- Ask HR who has done the job before and let them know what skill you are trying to acquire.
- When you hear names of individuals, ask around and see if they would make a good teacher. Can they communicate well? Are they patient? Do they have a desire to help others grow?
- Call and schedule a meeting. Ask them to help you over the course of a month to gain the skills you need. They can show you where to find information, give you a hands-on demonstration, or review some of your work and critique it for improvement.
- Follow up with a thank you after your first session with them and also send a formal thank you note when you are done the training that you agreed to.

To Find a Sponsor:

- Make a list of all of the key influencers in your organization when it comes to hiring, promotions, and training decisions. You can start by looking at titles, and understanding who attends certain meetings, who gets time at the microphone at big company events, and just by observing who is talking to whom in the parking lots.
- Consider who you have an existing relationship with.
- Consider who you could easily initiate a relationship with through being introduced by a mutual colleague.
- Do a little research on their career path and what roles they have held. See if you can understand who helped them in their career and find out the history of how they rose to the level they are at.
- Now think about what you would like. Maybe you wish to be selected for training, to be given an interview for a new role, or to be selected for a special high-profile project.
- Capture the reasons why you are interested and why you would be a great candidate.
- Book the meeting and make the pitch.
- Follow up with a thank you after your meeting even before you know if they will be a sponsor or not. Thank them for their time.
- Send a formal written thank you note when you know they have agreed to go to bat for you as your sponsor and stay in touch.

The next chapter shows you how to build on your learning plan with two of the most critical skills that are required for today's competitive work world: accelerating trust and building strong relationships. When you cultivate these key leadership competencies, you can navigate any organization and deliver results faster than ever before.

KEY POINTS FROM CHAPTER 5

- Strive to keep your skills competitive and marketable.
- Create a thorough skills inventory for yourself and find ways to fill in any gaps you discover.
- Commit to learning new skills and knowledge year round, at every opportunity.
- Practice techniques that keep your eyes open for new learning sessions so you can always stay ahead of the pack.
- Seek out a mentor whom you can ask advice from on a regular basis about your overall career path and life plan.
- Seek out a coach if you need coaching for specific skills you might be lacking.
- See if you can find a sponsor inside the company or organization who has your back and supports you.

Chapter 6

Cultivate Trusted Relationships

Your ability to establish working relationships quickly and effectively will allow you to navigate your workplace with ease and get things done. Once you are trusted you become a *driver of results*. It can supercharge your career, open doors, and completely change how you are perceived. Without question, the ability to build trust and credibility has become a key leadership competency in our world today. *It's a game-changer.*

Companies hire people who can establish trust at lightning speed, because in our intensely competitive world, trust is one of the best ways to keep customers, clients, and partners happy and committed to doing ongoing business with you. Not surprisingly then, companies today invest substantial training dollars to help their senior leaders understand how to build trust through times of change, like mergers and acquisitions, and across different cultures around the world.

Some people are natural collaborators, good at the personal side of relationships. They work with a philosophy of open and transparent communication, they address issues head on, and they know how to gain buy-in. These are *the special few*. They make it look easy and seem to have vast networks they can tap into at any time. They appear to have incredible instincts and confidence, and can make things happen quickly – get answers from the top, secure approvals for projects, and convince people to invest extra money when needed. While they make it look easy, the truth is that they *work really hard* to establish trust.

In this chapter we'll decode these successful behaviors and give you some tips on how you can accelerate trust and cultivate strong relationships that will be there for you whenever you need them.

Defining Trust in the Workplace

I believe that trust is a currency, meaning you can earn it and you can grow it, but you also have to safeguard it. Just like with your reputation, you have to *re-earn* trust all the time. You do this by displaying the right kind of key behaviors and actions consistently. This might sound simple enough to do, but it does take effort to go about building trust. The effort and investment is more than worth it however, especially when you do it in a very deliberate way.

First let's think about what trust *looks like* and why it is so important to constantly display trust-building behaviors and actions. This is what I call the ability to *accelerate trust*. Building and accelerating trust comes from the combination of three distinct things:

1 Your personal behavior.

2 Your track record of results.

3 Endorsements from your network.

This last point is why networking is so important when it comes to accelerating trust. Whenever people in positions of authority and credibility speak highly of you, their endorsement becomes an automatic ticket for entry into new work opportunities, even before your employers have seen you on that job.

Embody Personal Behaviors That Accelerate Trust

Let me share first about how your personal behaviors impact on trust. I'm talking here about how you conduct yourself which translates in your life to things like openness, transparency, honesty, collaboration, not gossiping, having a positive attitude, and using influence appropriately. You will be trusted more if you know how to hold a confidence and you have a good moral compass.

In order to accelerate trustworthiness, show respect to everyone, no matter their level in the organization. Never let yourself be seen as someone who treats people in positions of authority better than those who are working at other levels of the company.

This respect also extends to demonstrating *respect for yourself.* Therefore, be very careful about the stories you tell, the language you use, how you behave at company events (how late you stay, how much you drink), and what you post on social media sites. You can be your own worst enemy in terms of your personal credibility. Don't give the impression that there is one side of you at work, but that you hold a different level of values or ethics at home.

Communicate Effectively and Frequently

While on the job, strive to communicate and connect frequently with people who you need to maintain good working relationships with. Whether it's an update about the status of projects, information you have that others would value, or a note of thanks or congratulations – communicate, communicate, *communicate!*

When you are forthcoming with helpful information to assist colleagues, it boosts their confidence in you. They are also more likely to consider you a strong collaborator and team player.

Another sign of a strong communicator is someone who listens. When you actively feedback what someone is saying, they will feel heard. It demonstrates that you respect what the person has to say, and that you understand what they are trying to accomplish. We'll get more into strategic listening later in Chapter 8.

Being accessible is another guaranteed way to build trust. When others want to communicate with you, find ways to make time, and be responsive. Don't leave people hanging. This doesn't mean you have to jump every time someone wants time on your schedule, but if you want to build trust quickly, it's a good idea to send a reply within 24 hours.

Be Open and Transparent

Honesty is always important. Sharing your knowledge openly and directly is a surefire way to accelerate trust, especially with a new colleague or manager who needs to know important information to assess the landscape and opportunities for improvement.

And remember, what you don't say is just as important as what you do say. Nothing is worse than telling half the story, and having someone find out after the fact that you withheld some aspect of important information. Just imagine that someone in a position of trust in your company recommended a person for a job. They described the individual's past job experience, character, awards, and achievements, but they failed to mention that they were close personal friends who spent a lot of time outside of work in each other's company.

If this last point was revealed only after the person was hired, other team members who later find out could feel there was a conflict of interest. Trust would be eroded, teammates would be skeptical, and the new hire could face a tough start at the company. This all could have been avoided if the person making the recommendation had been open and honest, and disclosed all aspects of the situation.

Once you do have someone's trust, be sure to use any influence you have wisely. Don't abuse it by running to people (especially the boss) prematurely with information that is incomplete or not yours to share. No one appreciates a snitch. Most people can't recover from abusing a position of influence. They might gather more favor with the boss at that moment, but teammates will remember if you sold them out, and you will be shut out.

Keep Your Emotions in Check

Being hot-headed, gossiping, venting, shouting, walking around with a scowl on your face, or banging your fists on the table … all of these are negative behaviors that erode confidence and trust, and add nothing but stress to the workplace. They don't gain you anything other than a bad reputation, and people will not want to work closely with you.

Negative behavior tells other people that you are aren't a winner or a team player. This is not to say that you can't be passionate about something you believe in, but you need to be careful about how frequently you let your emotions go off the deep end. In the workplace, you will be valued more highly if you keep your cool, don't act arrogant, and if you are practical and open to ideas.

Don't hesitate to say you are sorry if you've crossed the line, let someone down, or made a mistake. Being able to apologize sincerely is a sign of maturity and will tell others that you know that you have room for improvement. It also demonstrates that you will attempt to do better next time.

Be Open Minded

Likewise, be willing to compromise and negotiate. When you are open to new ideas and flexible, you will be able to gather honest feedback and have more information to draw from when you do need to make decisions. On the other hand, if you are too closely married to your own ideas, other colleagues may decide that you are pushy, a poor listener, and unwilling to consider other people's viewpoints. In order to build trust, you need to give a little and help other people with their goals.

These may all sound like simple things, but I'm always amazed how often people are oblivious to the behaviors they exhibit that erode trust. This next point keeps coming up, but is worth saying once more: *self-awareness is a powerful tool.* If you have habits or behaviors that are not serving you, you can change them up and it's time to do so.

Maintain a Strong Track Record of Proven Results

Once you enter the world of work, commit to developing a strong track record of proven results and become a collaborator that everyone can count on. Coming up in Chapter 8, I will discuss *delivering results* in detail, but for now let me share a few more ways you can build a strong track record quickly, even if you are new to a workplace.

First, be accountable. This means that you take ownership and demonstrate that you are holding yourself responsible. This can be shown quickly, with a simple statement like, "I'll take accountability for that. I'll get the information needed and be back to the group in two days." It's action-oriented, specific, and shows you're not going to pass the buck. You're happy to take on a main role.

Once you do make a commitment, be sure to follow through. People need to know that you are dependable and that if you say you're going to do something, you do it. If you can over-deliver on deadlines or quality, that's even better. If someone drops the ball, I've heard them say, "Oh, I'm still learning," like it's some kind of honeymoon phase because they are new at the job. That's really no longer acceptable. In today's competitive workplace, it's expected you will deliver right away, even if you are learning about the industry or the job. If for some reason you can't follow through on something you've committed to do, give lots of notice with a good reason why.

Try to share information in a timely fashion because most people don't like surprises in the workplace. And use your judgment about what might need to be escalated to management. People will appreciate it if you speak up and share what you know, rather than waiting until something goes seriously off-track and admitting later, "Oh yeah, I heard about that." Sharing information at the right time helps people make better decisions.

When you add all this up, building trust means that you can be counted on to do your part at all times. If you're asked to be a member of a team or committee, step up and offer to take on some of the work. If everything has been assigned already, let people know you can be available as back up, a second set of eyes, or to take on something specific next time around.

Endorsements from Your Network

It's clear that a big part of accelerating trust is your behavior and your track record of good work. The final element that can catapult you from an unknown newbie to a trusted individual is an endorsement from someone who is widely respected and credible. What other people say about you is critical. It can open doors, ease fears, and inspire others. This is precisely why you need to have a strong network.

When it comes to preparing for your future, networking is as important as financial planning, taking care of your health, or landing that dream job or client. *Why?* Because the relationships you cultivate now will last for years – decades even – and will determine what opportunities come your way in life. Strangely, most people avoid networking or are reluctant participants at best.

I was surprised with the results when my company conducted a survey on this subject. It showed that 85% of respondents in their 20s said they don't network, or only network if the opportunity presents itself. Furthermore, only 28% of respondents over the age of 30 said they proactively network. This is such a shame because *not networking* is really a lost opportunity.

I realize of course that many people may feel awkward, shy, or insecure in crowds or among strangers, but the reality is that networking is an essential skill, especially now with technology everywhere. You just can't accomplish the same things when you are tied to your gadgets 24/7, that you can through social interaction and networking with your peers and other industry leaders. In fact, networking is so important that many companies train their employees how to do it more effectively.

Even if you are not a social butterfly, you can become much better at personal interactions if you just practice regularly. It's a skill that you can master and below are some pointers to flex your personal communication muscles.

ESSENTIAL EXERCISE

IMPROVE YOUR NETWORK

When it comes to networking, it's about the *quality* of the connections, not the *quantity*. When building your network, remember that you are seeking to establish your reputation with people who can support you. The objective is not just to collect a bunch of miscellaneous names or business cards.

Think about networking as an investment, an asset that you bring to your job and to your organization. It's a strength you can speak about in a job interview. Networks also allow you to access new information, open doors, augment your learning, and be resourceful in all kinds of ways. Once you give yourself the gift of networking, it will reward you over your entire lifetime.

Here are some strategic actions you can take to build a strong network of contacts you can call on and tap into whenever needed.

1 *Maintain business friendships or rekindle old ties.* You can begin with the alumni group from your college or university and include your professors and former classmates. Then branch out into any relevant volunteer groups or previous employers and employees you worked with in the past. Then build your circle by using social media and join online groups that are relevant to your interests.

2 *Be aware that you have to give in order to get.* Networking with people is less about your interests than theirs, so find ways to bring value to them and stand out in their minds when they first meet you. For example, you can send someone a book you think they'd like, write a nice note to recognize someone's accomplishments, or just take the time to pen a thank you note when someone gives you advice, an interview (even if you didn't get the job), or if they taught you something new.

3 *Actively attend networking events.* Take advantage of events and prepare ahead of time. Be sure to take business cards. If you don't have a job yet, create a personal card with your name and contact information on it. Get there early because it's much easier to start a conversation than to join one already in progress once groups have formed. Be prepared with your elevator pitch and your personal story, but don't monopolize the conversation. Ask questions and be genuinely interested in the other people's work and why they are there. In doing so, you will learn valuable insights about the people you meet, their priorities, and their networks – *which could someday be your networks*. Make a note to follow-up if you do discover some good connections.

4 *Be opportunistic since people gather in many different places.* In your effort to be noticed within your company or industry, don't be blind to everyday opportunities to make connections. For example, pay attention to who might be sitting next to you at a fundraising dinner. Make a point to stay after an interesting lecture and thank the speaker so you can begin to establish new ties. If you hear about an interesting event or activity, ask someone how you can get an invitation. Opportunities to meet new people present themselves every day. Learn to recognize them and act on them.

5 *Mix it up and follow up.* It can be tempting to stay in a familiar circle, but force yourself to get outside your comfort zone. Approach a new group or person with a warm smile and handshake, and ask them about their work. When you get home, write a short note saying something like: "We met at the networking event last night. I really admire your work and wonder if you would be available to meet with me to offer me some career advice. I think I could learn a lot from you." *Presto! You've made a connection.*

REAL LIFE LESSON

ACCELERATING TRUST IN A VIRTUAL WORLD

Not everyone you work with or network with lives in your hometown so sometimes you have to get very creative to make meaningful connections. This story is about a young woman who shows how she dealt with a number of changes while being in a virtual work environment.

When Monica moved out of state, she was thrilled when her employer agreed that she could continue to work with the company from her new home office. She knew there were some pitfalls to being a virtual employee on a daily basis, such as the fact that she'd have to work harder to be known and trusted by management and by her in-office colleagues.

The first year was easy because the team at work and her boss all knew her very well. But when she got a new manager through a company restructuring, she knew she was then at a disadvantage. Her closest teammate Stephanie, whom she had known for years and who was her eyes and ears at the company offices, also left in that same shuffle for another part of the organization, so Monica felt far away and rather vulnerable indeed.

She decided she would make the best of it so she put a strategy together to increase her visibility and accelerate the trust relationship with her new manager, Ingrid, and the new executive assistant, Craig. She made an excuse to visit her old stomping grounds and in fact, she stayed in the city with her friend Stephanie which was a nice bonus and meant she wasn't out of pocket on hotel costs. The flight was a personal expense, but Monica felt confident it would be money well spent to reestablish herself within the new environment at the company.

Monica booked her trip and timed it to coincide with when they had just filled Stephanie's position. Monica went into the office Monday to Friday that week and took up an empty cubicle in the bullpen making herself at home. Monica checked in with Craig, the new bosses' assistant, each morning to say hi and to give him a run-down of her intended activities for the day.

While speaking with Craig, she requested a meeting with Ingrid too and she got two hours of face-time with her. Monica took that time to share recent accomplishments, present upcoming challenges, and talk about potential solutions that she had already worked out in advance that she wanted to get buy-in for. Ingrid was impressed that Monica was so forward-thinking and seemed to have such a good handle on the workflow and requirements.

In addition, Monica spent a great deal of time that week working closely with the new recruit, Patrick, and showing him around the office and the job. They even went out one night to a favorite nearby restaurant with some other colleagues for dinner and a catch-up gab session. Since Craig was also new to the company, Monica made a point to invite him as well, and he enjoyed meeting some more members of the department on a social basis.

Monica and Patrick met with IT several times that week to request and work through some software improvements that would help them become more efficient in their joint project work. And Monica made a point to figure out which aspects of the job Patrick preferred and excelled at. Monica happily agreed to take on some of his less favorite tasks so she further earned his respect for being so flexible and helpful.

At the end of the week, when Monica stopped by to say goodbye and thank you to Craig, she couldn't help but smile when he told her the latest news from the boss. Apparently Ingrid told Craig that she thought the week Monica had spent at head office was very valuable. Ingrid thought it would be a good idea to do a week like that once a quarter to coincide with the usual strategic planning and management review process so that Monica could attend those in person.

The travel and accommodation costs would be built into the budget moving forward, and Monica was happy to feel freshly reconnected to the job that she loved. Virtual employee or not, she was once again an established and valuable member of the team. It had been the best five days she had spent in a long time.

ESSENTIAL EXERCISE

STAY CONNECTED IN A VIRTUAL WORLD

If you've never been part of a virtual workplace team, there's every expectation you will be at some point. With technology, you can be connected and productive from just about anywhere in the modern world. While it's nice to have flexibility, the truth is that working effectively can be a challenge when you've never met your colleagues or even your manager or client in person. Standing out and creating a name for yourself can sometimes feel next to impossible.

After all, studies show that people who get repeated exposure to senior executives are the ones who get promoted. The more you interact with senior executives, the more chances you'll have to make a good impression and open doors for career opportunities.

If you're working on a virtual team or with a client that is located a distance from you, you're no doubt wondering how to get more exposure especially when your peers or competitors are in much closer physical proximity. Monica used several good strategies and here are some more tips to help you get noticed when you work in a virtual environment.

1 *You must have some face-time.* At some point, you need to connect with your boss and your teammates in person. This can be a challenge with travel freezes, but try. Encourage your manager to call a team session. Drop by the head office if you are on vacation nearby. Persuade your manager to let you attend a work trip to learn a new skill, deliver a presentation, or add value in some way beyond networking.

2 *Make the best of virtual meetings and video conference calls.* Use these wisely. Call in early and greet others as they join. Speak up, ask questions, and offer input. Make sure your voice is heard. Videoconferencing is the next best thing to being there in person. It's particularly good for one-to-one discussions or small groups where people can see and hear each other clearly, plus you can gesture and show examples of things to each other.

3 *Take photos and share stories.* Snap a few pictures of your project or your work team, and send them to the boss with some statistics about what's happening. Leaders in head office appreciate seeing what's going on out in the field and this allows management to stay connected to the real-time data.

4 *Become uber-strategic in your networking.* Think about who you need to get in front of, and reach out to them to share your knowledge and insights on a topic that is important to them. Add value, offer to lead projects, and share relevant industry reports. Become the "go-to" person in the field that leaders can rely upon for insight and action.

5 *Book a recurring weekly time to speak with one or two key contacts if you can.* If you have key colleagues that you work with on ongoing projects, set a given time each week where you are committed to connect, such as every Tuesday at 8 a.m. That way, you both know you'll always have a touch point with each other and you can make notes of outstanding issues, concerns, or new ideas that you can continue to share consistently every single week. Sometimes you or they might have to miss an online meeting, but when the appointment is recurring, you know you can always catch up the following week.

ESSENTIAL EXERCISE

IDENTIFY YOUR MOST IMPORTANT WORK RELATIONSHIPS

For this *Essential Exercise*, think about the many different hats that you wear and write them down. Be creative and list all the ways you spend your time. Consider your day job, personal outside projects, an entrepreneurial venture, volunteer work, community activism, past work colleagues, special interest groups, important family connections, and don't forget any alumni or student groups you belong to.

For each hat you wear, think about the *trusted relationships* that you need to cultivate. Then beside each group or activity that you have on your list, write down a couple of important names of people you wish to keep in touch with.

Think of ways that you can *stay top of mind* with each of these important people and write down the action steps you could do to put yourself on their radar. There are many creative ways you can connect that would be of benefit to them, like sending them a link to an industry article, offering to meet for a coffee to get an update on their latest project, or writing them an encouraging note to say you're looking forward to seeing them at an upcoming event.

Consider what you can do each week or each month to continue to cultivate trust with these individuals and *then do it*. Review your list at least once a week to keep on top of changes and to record new ideas. Once you make this a habit, it becomes second nature to stay connected and I guarantee you, this system will pay you back exponentially.

In the next chapter, you'll explore how to speak up for yourself in a confident and consistent way. You'll learn the best ways to present your ideas, how to avoid pitfalls that can erode trust, and find ways to deliver your message effectively.

KEY POINTS FROM CHAPTER 6

- Learn how to *accelerate trust* because it's a key leadership competency in the new world.
- Trust is a combination of your personal behaviors, your proven track record, and endorsements from your network.
- Trusted relationships will help you navigate organizations better and deliver results faster.
- Actively network inside and outside of your organization.
- Build good relationships with peers, managers, senior leaders, and industry contacts.
- Authentically connect with people. Getting along well is not just a one-way exercise; you must learn to *give and take*.
- To accelerate trust in a virtual workplace, pay extra attention to the creative ways you can promote yourself and your contributions.

CHAPTER 7

FIND YOUR VOICE AND OWN IT

In Chapter 3, you learned to understand your natural personality strengths and discovered ways to build on those. Throughout the whole book so far, you have been finding out more about who you are and what you are most comfortable doing, so now is the logical time to *step fully into that space*. In this chapter, you'll find out ways to embrace your gifts, find your voice, and own it. Then in Chapter 8, you're going to bring together all these skills to *deliver results* in a powerful way.

For now, the focus is on boosting your confidence and empowering you to make a bigger contribution to the workplace. You want to get noticed as someone who does their homework, spends appropriate time thinking and preparing, and as a result, brings added value to projects and meetings.

You really have to know the best ways to present yourself in meetings because it's one of the easiest ways to assert yourself. Yet, so many people sit in meetings without saying a word. Maybe you are the silent type so you know what I mean.

You may think that you are flying under the radar, but rest assured, people are noticing if you appear to be making a contribution or not.

But even worse than not speaking up is the person who does try to say something but prefaces their comments with self-defeating language that erodes their credibility. We've all heard people start off a very good idea with, "I may be wrong, but …" or "I've never done this before, but …." What the rest of the meeting hears is: *this person has no idea what they are talking about.* If you have ever used this kind of self-defeating talk, I would advise that you catch yourself and break that habit before it gets too engrained.

There are so many better ways to demonstrate that you might not be an expert but that you have a solid idea that is worthy of consideration by your teammates. Maybe you'd like to suggest some innovative approach, call it XYZ, but you don't have every detail worked out. What if you said it this way: "I've been doing some reading on this topic because I know it's very important to our team. It would appear that some of the best companies in this field are doing XYZ. That could be a very good approach for us to consider in this instance. Even if we don't follow this path fully, we'll learn about the best practices and gain some important insights." *See the difference?* You sound far more confident.

With a little practice using some of the tips and techniques from this chapter, you can break free of approaches that don't really serve you and replace them with solid practices that will help you find your unique voice and really own it.

How to Shine In Meetings

If you are new to a formal workplace, you may not have a lot of experience with business meetings. While many employees dread meetings and consider them a waste of time, they continue to be used as the primary means to discuss topics and make decisions.

The quality of a meeting depends largely on the meeting organizer, but as a participant, you have an important role to ensure success. Basically, you are responsible to prepare properly for the meeting, speak up while attending when appropriate, seek clarity for anything you don't understand, and then follow up after the meeting on aspects that you asked to take on or which have been assigned to you.

As for preparing for a meeting there are three steps. First, if material was circulated in advance, *read it*. This is not only a sign of respect to your colleagues who invested hours to prepare it, but it will give you a strong advantage. You'll improve your status just by knowing the content because many people are too rushed or unorganized to digest the information upfront.

Second, take time to review the agenda and understand the goal of the meeting. Is it to create awareness, come to a consensus, or make a decision or recommendation? Third, know who is attending. Meetings are a great way to get to know more colleagues and expand your network so pay attention to who has been invited.

Be prepared to speak up as a meeting participant, so you can make a positive contribution. This can be challenging if other individuals monopolize the discussion or if you are an introvert and can't find the right opening to voice your thoughts. If you want to be sure you have something to contribute, make notes as you review the material in advance and commit to share your thoughts on some aspect of the data that you read.

For example, you can ask a question about costs, customers, risk, partners, competition, or geography. But be succinct and to the point or you'll likely get interrupted by some of the more dominant or experienced personalities.

Learning to Speak Up and Follow Up

In most meetings, you don't need to wait until it's your turn. *It won't be your turn.* You need to *take* your turn. Focus on doing this with grace and be well mannered, but make sure you find a way to offer your viewpoint in a professional and confident way. As long as you don't nag or constantly interrupt, you'll be OK. You have a right to be heard and after the first few times, it should come easier.

If you need a clarification on something, chances are other meeting participants do too. Ask the meeting organizer or presenter for more detail if it's warranted. Another great way to speak up and help all the meeting attendees is to ask for a quick recap of the action items just as the meeting draws to a close. No meeting should ever adjourn without outcomes and next steps being agreed upon by all.

There are two main steps in the follow-up process after a meeting. First, find an appropriate time to thank the meeting organizer. You will find that sending an email or visiting the organizer personally after the meeting has adjourned will have a greater positive impact than a quick "thank you" as you exit the room. Express how much you appreciated being included in the meeting and why you found it valuable. Second and most importantly, be sure to follow up promptly on any actions that were assigned to you or that you volunteered for.

While all this might seem like simple meeting etiquette, it's surprising how many people in today's workplace don't prepare or contribute and who don't give proper courtesy to the meeting organizers. You can outshine just about everyone by following the simple steps above and setting an example for others.

REAL LIFE LESSON

GETTING YOUR MESSAGE HEARD

Everyone was trying to find a way to distinguish themselves in the newly acquired company. Michael and Maddie were two of the many people jockeying for attention and wanting to be heard. They knew they needed to get some airtime with the new leader in order to illustrate their strengths and their value to the new leadership. *But how?* No one really knew anything about the new leader except his name was Mr. Boss and he wore a nice suit.

Michael chose to send an email to Mr. Boss with a pleasant note. It read something like: "Welcome aboard. I appreciated meeting you at our recent team function. Please don't hesitate to let me know if I can do anything to help you with your new role. Thanks, Michael."

He got a quick reply: "Thanks Michael. We've got a lot of work ahead of us. I need to be able to count on every single employee to keep our company strong and performing well against the competition. Signed, Mr. Boss."

Maddie had attended the same team meeting but she didn't email right away. Instead she called Mr. Boss' Executive Assistant (EA) and introduced herself. She explained that at a recent team meeting, Mr. Boss asked everyone for insights on how the company could perform better. Mr. Boss made it clear that since he was new to this acquired company, he was counting on the eyes and ears on the ground to keep him apprised of potential opportunities.

Maddie explained to the EA that she had very good background information on trends that she thought he would appreciate seeing, but she wasn't certain of the best way to convey her thoughts. She asked the EA what communication preferences Mr. Boss had because she wanted to respect those.

In particular, Maddie asked, does he read his email personally? Does he accept text messages on his mobile phone? What about booking a meeting – is that even possible? Perhaps there is a possibility for a call after he's had a chance to see what she's prepared? Maddie underscored that she wants to be very respectful of his time and priorities.

Maddie learned from the EA that Mr. Boss was extremely busy, with a demanding travel schedule. Given the newly acquired company, his email box was jam-packed and he really couldn't keep up with it. However, the EA said that since it sounded important – and because the EA and Maddie now had a rapport – they agreed on five things:

1 Maddie would send a quick text message to Mr. Boss to say thanks for the meeting, glad you are our new boss – email coming with the info you asked for. Maddie did this, and included a group photo from the team function with a personal notation: *I'm second from the left.*

2 Maddie would send the email with the details to Mr. Boss and copy the EA. The EA agreed to print it off and place it on his desk.

3 The email from Maddie would have all of the pertinent contact information on it should Mr. Boss want to call in order to dig deeper into the facts and trends that Maddie had pulled together and sent (her email, phone number, and cell were all clear on the email).

4 Maddie also asked the EA to program her cell phone number and contact info into the contact list that the EA had created for the boss, because Maddie had a feeling they'd be working closely in future. The EA did that for her.

5 Maddie thanked the EA and told her not to hesitate to reach out, because Maddie was happy to be her local contact on the ground should she need anything at all.

Maddie got a call from Mr. Boss within a few days to discuss the email, and Michael was left wondering why she got all the visibility with the new leader and he did not.

To Send or *Not to Send*, That is the Question

I think just about everyone worries about when to send emails, text messages, or join a company chat. But it all comes down to knowing your audience. I've heard many people tell me that they sit in front of their computer screen for hours, wondering whether or not to send a note to the boss. *Will they look stupid? Will their manager even read it?*

Any insecurity that is felt can be due to many factors, a whole host of things that could include lack of confidence, lack of clarity, or being unfamiliar with the individual's schedule or communication preferences. But the key to you using your voice effectively in the workplace is to know your audience. It can take some time and finesse to do your homework but as you can see in the case of Maddie and Michael above, the time and strategy that Maddie used to figure out how to reach Mr. Boss was time well spent.

This matter of what to send, when, and how is obviously also related to the content in the previous chapter about cultivating trusted relationships. These are all examples of how to find your voice and own it. What it really comes down to is this: if you want to have your message received properly, be sure to send it the way that the recipient likes to get it. When you do, you'll have a much higher chance of it being read and acted upon.

ESSENTIAL EXERCISE

PUT FACTS BEFORE FEELINGS

Whether you are in a meeting, pitching ideas to your boss, or leading your teammates through some information they need to know, *facts matter*. Leaders in organizations need to make hundreds of decisions a day. They need to be able to count on the information you present. They will repeat parts of the facts that make up the case, and send that factual summary up the line, so you need to know what you are saying is true. You don't want any misinformation from you to embarrass them or lead to poor decision-making at the top.

Here are few tips to get it right and use your voice effectively when you are raising points and pitching ideas at work. There is more about this in the next chapter but this will get you thinking about how to have your voice heard and respected.

- *Be Careful of the Rumor Mill.* It's easy to get pulled into gossip and the rumor mill, especially during times of change or uncertainty. If you are feeling uneasy and there are some negative emotions floating around, you are more likely to have your concerns and feelings amplified by listening to unsubstantiated talk, informal feed-back, and out of control stories. Remain calm and consider what you hear rationally, rather than getting swept up by what "everyone is saying." It's quite likely just a small number of people have that opinion and while they are being very loud and upset about it, it doesn't mean that what they are saying is universally accepted or even true. And be careful what you say to management in those cases because your credibility will be in jeopardy if there is no real basis for your claims. Exaggeration is a surefire way to erode trust.

- **Pay Attention to Influencers.** It is appropriate to bring forward people's opinions if they are influencers or key stakeholders however. For example, if someone has gone on record in a meeting, letter, memo, or other published source and they are stating information about an investment or change in strategic direction, then you can share that as long as you are not breaking any confidences. When you quote legitimate experts or sources, it strengthens your position and boosts the points you are making.

- **Use Only Relevant Data.** Be factual. Leaders want facts, trends, and objective statements, not just vague opinions. Before you send off an email or walk into a meeting with a big pronouncement, do a little homework. What are the results saying on a particular project milestone? How many sales did we win or lose this week? What is the key driver of our success and how do we learn from that? Leaders want *information* they can use to see if there are trends that can be applied to other parts of the organization. They want *insights* to help them avoid risk. But any stories or examples have to be based on verifiable facts.

R E A L   L I F E   L E S S O N

S O R T I N G   O U T   R E A L I T Y   F R O M   F A N T A S Y

When I was leading a communications department, people would constantly come to me and tell me how messages were being received. I would hear things like, "Everyone is talking about that latest message," and how terrible it was that *so and so* said *this or that*. My response was always, "Who is *everyone?* How *many* is everyone?"

The answer was usually something crazy such as, "the people in the elevator." OK. Well, only so many people fit in an elevator. You can hardly call that *everyone*. And while I tried to take every comment seriously, some reports were just too supercharged with emotion for me to believe that there was a massive revolt afoot.

I think you will find that often when there is too much drama in a story, the messenger is the one who loses credibility. Just about every time when I looked into those situations, it was a lot of smoke and mirrors but no real substance. Most often it was just a case of emotions running amok.

That being said, we live in a world where claims and stories can quickly go viral and take on a life of their own. It can be difficult to get to the truth, but you need to try. You want to be on top of things so you're able to tell what needs immediate attention and what is merely a distraction. Seek out verification from another credible source whenever possible.

❖

ESSENTIAL EXERCISE

NEGOTIATE DIFFICULT MEETINGS

This *Essential Exercise* will help you maintain a calm and professional demeanor. Emotional evenness is important because when you remain practical, fact-based, calm, and balanced, you will always gain greater respect and trust. You don't want to react in a knee-jerk, rapid fire, exaggerated, or emotional way because that sends the opposite impression.

My advice is to practice upfront how you will use your voice and your tone if a meeting gets off track for any reason. When you practice in advance, you will know what to do if you are challenged or have to deal with dissenters. Here are some suggestions to consider.

- If someone challenges you in a meeting, you can say: "Thanks, I hadn't thought of that. Maybe we can meet afterward to talk about this some more. It sounds like you've got some valuable insights we could build on, but for now, let's stay on track."
- If someone disagrees with you in a meeting, you can say: "OK. I understand and respect that. Is there any missing information I could share that might help make you more comfortable?"
- If the meeting gets off track completely, you might bring it back to focus by saying: "I'm glad we've got so much interest in this topic. I'm mindful of the time and want to respect everyone's schedule today. Madam Chair, may I proceed with my final few points?"

Real Life Lesson

Setting Up a Schedule of Wins

The senior leadership team met on a Monday morning, just like they always did. Each department head reviewed their team's current activities, reporting on how well they were achieving their goals. This meeting gave everyone a chance to stay connected and to understand any new challenges or opportunities that surfaced.

This day, the head of the Strategy department, Claire, indicated that a smaller company in their same field was looking for a buyer, and that Claire's group had been doing some research about whether or not it would be a suitable acquisition. She reported on the key facts of the company: number of employees, customer base, revenues, branch locations, systems, and the financial aspects of a potential purchase.

The President had been aware of this activity and had made up his mind that this would be a formidable addition to help them grow their company. He decided to establish a project team that could go on-site and meet with the owners and do some more homework before they put a formal purchase offer on the table. He gave the team two months to complete their work and report back to him with their recommendation.

The team was made up of various departments that would have to assess this potential acquisition. Finance would look into the company's books and understand if there were any issues. Human Resources would assess the workforce and its leaders, and see if there were any issues in terms of labor agreements, workplace policies, or culture. Information Technology would assess their IT systems and see if they would easily integrate. And the Legal Department would assess existing agreements, conflicts or risks. Each department would assign a representative, who would in turn report to Claire as the head of Strategy over the next two months.

Claire called a meeting of all of the representatives and told them that she expected them to carry out their work, and report to her regularly – as they saw fit and however they liked (email, face-to-face meeting, or phone call) – so she could hear about any issues and stay on top of their progress. She advised them that in four weeks – half way through the project – she would be meeting with the President to give him an interim status update and reassure him how things were proceeding.

Claire knew everyone would have a different approach and she was right. Lloyd was assigned from IT. He left the meeting and went about his business. He booked a flight to the company, arrived onsite and spent the first week there looking at the systems and trying to understand how things might integrate. It was important for him to know how the inventory systems could talk to each other, how customers would be transitioned into a common database, how invoicing could be migrated, how bills would be presented and so on. He was very busy and totally immersed himself in the challenge. He figured he could get the work done in about six weeks and he would update Claire when he had finished his assessment at that point. That would still leave two weeks before the final recommendation was due to the President.

Jeff was assigned from HR and took a different approach. He had only worked on one acquisition before and in that case he shadowed a more senior person so he could learn the process. This time, he was on his own. He wanted to do a good job and impress Claire. He knew she had the President's ear and if he did well on this assignment, he could potentially secure her as a mentor or even a sponsor in the future.

He left the meeting and went to his desk to map out a timeline. He knew that setting key milestones would keep everyone focused and would increase the likelihood they would meet their deadlines. So Jeff built a framework to help the HR group communicate their process with confidence and credibility. It looked something like this.

In Week 1, Jeff focused on introductions and data collection. He initiated contact and introduced himself to the people he would be working with on the other side of the table. He would share his timeline with the HR people at the company they were considering purchasing, along with key milestones, and request that all information be forwarded to him by the end of the day on Thursdays, so he could email a report to Claire each Friday afternoon.

For Week 2, he would focus on research and evaluate the labor agreements, special work contracts, organizational charts, employee policies, and compensation schemes. During Week 3, he scheduled a number of onsite interviews so he could spend the week clarifying any questions that surfaced from the material review. In particular, he would interview the senior leaders and complete a cultural fit questionnaire so he could flag any concerns about personalities or practices that might get in the way of a smooth integration.

During Week 4, his focus was to get an Interim Summary Report produced and sent to Claire. Jeff remembered that she said she would be meeting with the President then and he wanted to make sure that she would be able to convey – with confidence – that Jeff's work was strong and on track.

Jeff pulled his timeline plans together into a professional document and asked for a meeting with Claire. She liked his proactive approach. He also asked Claire if there was anything she thought he was missing, which gave her an opportunity to redirect him or expand his scope of work before they even started. Jeff made sure they were aligned and that they agreed on what he was going to deliver. He said he would send her a regular Friday email that would let her know of any additional progress or issues that had surfaced in the previous seven days.

What Jeff did was set up a series of *quick wins* that would get Claire onboard with his plan and establish himself to be profiled at the upcoming mid-point meeting. He knew that if he did well on his Interim Summary Report at the four-week mark, Claire would share it with the President because she had a reputation for giving credit where it was due.

Note that Jeff designed his work flow with weekly goals (which he broke down into daily checklists) so he could leverage the timing of the meeting with the President, as well as build in lots of buffer time for Weeks 5 to 8 so he could deal with anything he might uncover or in case anyone missed any deadlines.

He discovered in the interviews that there were additional work contracts that his counterpart in HR didn't even know about. The buffer that he built in gave him time to review those carefully without those surprises being crammed into the last two weeks of the whole assignment.

Jeff stayed true to his word and sent Claire an email update every Friday with a simple one-page summary of what he had accomplished. In doing so, every week he delivered a "win" and reinforced Claire's confidence in him. Jeff also copied his own head of HR to ensure she was informed and pleased with the progress.

Jeff used language like: "As we discussed, I have implemented a timeline to ensure we stay on track and meet the expectations of the evaluation. I have held myself and the team accountable to deliver on key milestones each week so that we can maintain the project pace. While it is ambitious, I am pleased to report that for the third week in a row, we've met our goals. Three unexpected matters have surfaced and I will take responsibility to dig into these further in Weeks 5 and 6. I'll continue to bring any other issues to your attention so that you are fully informed. Thanks once again for the opportunity to work on this exciting project."

Meanwhile, Claire had not heard from Lloyd who was overseeing the IT side of the company they were considering acquiring. She had heard that he had travelled to the company to do onsite system assessments, but that was all she knew. She called Lloyd a week before her meeting with the President to ask how he was doing. He said it all was under control and that he expected they would have to maintain separate IT systems for a few months – maybe even up to a year – after the acquisition.

Upon hearing this, she asked Lloyd for specifics about how many systems this impacted, an estimate of the integration time and cost, and how big the IT team was there. Most importantly, she wanted to know how they could make it absolutely seamless for customers. They could not afford to lose any new customers to the competition while they sorted out and integrated the two IT systems.

Lloyd was a bit overwhelmed. He was not prepared to discuss all of these detailed realities because he was still looking at the systems and testing whether or not they could talk to each other. Lloyd realized that if he and Claire had met earlier that her expectations would have been made clearer.

Still Lloyd remained pretty confident he could hit the two-month mark and provide everything she was asking for by that time, but there was no way he could give Claire the level of detail she seemed to suddenly want in time for the four-week check-in meeting with the President. Without the specific details, Lloyd thought that she might end up conveying some concern about his progress. He called his manager, the head of IT, and told her that he had a feeling Claire was unhappy and that she might want to brace herself for questions from the President.

Lloyd realized too late that all this stress could have been avoided by designing his workflow in a different way. He would have been better off setting up key milestones each week and making a point to report to Claire each week about his successes and challenges. That way, he would have known sooner that her main focus was on customer retention and not just the mechanics of the IT integration itself.

At the four-week mark, Claire sang the praises of Jeff and the HR team at the new company because she knew exactly where they were at and that they had delivered results each week, which impressed both Claire and the President. Challenges had been flagged each week and were being dealt with promptly.

But on the IT side, she only had vague cautions to report and no real data which didn't sit nearly as well with the President. Claire was disappointed that IT had dragged her down and she realized that she needed to manage all this more closely. So she set up calls each week during the last four weeks of the assessment and insisted that each representative call in with a detailed update so there would be no more unpleasant and unexpected surprises in the remaining month of the assessment.

ESSENTIAL EXERCISE

EARN THE CREDIT YOU DESERVE

An important way for you to use your voice is to make sure that you are receiving appropriate credit for the value and results that you bring to an organization. Here are some practical ways to ensure that your manager and other decision-makers understand the positive impact you are making.

- When a new initiative is starting, get in early if you can. Demonstrate you are working diligently on the new priorities that you are being assigned. This will help you create a positive image of yourself as someone who is proactive, conscientious, and accountable.
- Be prepared for all meetings and discussions. Bring relevant data, explain what you are working on, and how you have creatively approached the issue. Have solutions ready in advance.
- Design your workflow so that you can secure a "quick win" at the start, and then create an ongoing "series of wins" by assigning realistic key milestones to yourself along the way. Once you achieve them, you can share the successes with your manager in weekly team meetings either face-to-face or by phone or video.
- It's always good to show your boss that you think in an organized way and you can do this by setting goals, and then stretching yourself and your team to reach those goals. Reporting on your goals and the team's goals will demonstrate that you hold yourself accountable and are making a consistent contribution.

- Keep track of the highlights of your projects and how they are supporting the overall strategy of the company. Quantify your results as much as you can. Share these results on a monthly or quarterly basis with your manager and show up to the meeting prepared with a written report that demonstrates linkages between your results and the organization's macro goals.

The next chapter will show you how to tap into your trusted relationships to demonstrate that you can deliver results and handle even more responsibility. Building your name and credibility as a leader depends on how well you interact with your colleagues, prepare for big moments, and keep projects moving forward, while at the same time linking your results to the bigger picture and getting recognized for your hard work.

KEY POINTS FROM CHAPTER 7

- Commit to preparing and contributing actively in all meetings you attend.
- Use meetings with your boss or top executives as key moments to advance your ideas and objectives.
- Stop any self-defeating behavior or statements. Instead, strive to be definitive and confident.
- Be factual. Leaders want facts, trends, and objective statements (not just vague opinions).
- Don't exaggerate or overstate your points because this will impact your credibility.
- Understand your audience. Put yourself in their shoes. Deliver messages in the way they would like to hear them, not in the way you want to deliver them. Be succinct and crisp.
- Set yourself up for a quick win first and then a series of ongoing wins along the way. Communicate these to ensure that you are seen as a person who can be counted on.

CHAPTER 8

DELIVER RESULTS

The fundamental reason that you will advance within your career is because people believe you can be counted on to achieve results. Let's break down this statement, since there are two critical parts to it. First, you have to be *able to achieve results* individually and by being part of a team.

The second part of the statement involves *perception*. People have to believe that you can deliver. Perception counts for a lot, so it's not enough to just consistently contribute good work. You also have to find ways to *get credit for your hard work* if you want to be given greater responsibilities and qualify to be promoted.

There are six key characteristics of a person who delivers results in a workplace. By the end of this chapter, you will fully understand each of these characteristics so you can use them to build your name and credibility as a leader. I'm also going to give you strategies so you will know how to secure the credit you deserve and be perceived in the best possible light. Specifically, here are the six points you may want to work on so everyone around you will know you can deliver results:

1 Develop a strong sense of ownership and accountability.

2 Become highly responsive and direct.

3 Show that you are intellectually curious.

4 Learn how to build consensus.

5 Become a strategic listener.

6 Learn how to paint a vision and sell ideas.

Develop a Strong Sense of Ownership and Accountability

If you are going to deliver results that get noticed, you have to care. Let me rephrase that: You have to care *a lot*. You have to feel a genuine sense of ownership about your work duties and take pride in the contribution you are making. The outcome has to matter to you.

Look around your office or workplace and you can tell who the highly accountable people are by the way they talk. You'll hear them say things like: "We'll figure this out. We can do this," and "Let's break this down into activities and timelines, roles and responsibilities." You'll also notice that successful and accountable people honor their word. If they say they are going to do something, *they do it*, and if they run into a roadblock, they provide the team or the boss with enough upfront notice and a logical rationale as to why it's not going to get done on schedule.

These are the people who also offer alternative solutions because they are driven to find ways to deliver and succeed. They take seriously what it is that they are getting paid to do, and understand how their work contributes to the bigger operation and overall strategic goals.

Now contrast these traits with someone considerably less successful. You know the kind of person I mean, someone who wanders aimlessly, has to be reminded of their commitments, and who is indifferent about things because they think that every matter is *someone else's problem*. How many times have you heard a colleague say, "That decision is above my pay band. Someone higher up gets paid to worry about those things." Hopefully you aren't the one saying this. This kind of thinking is the kiss of death for your career. It means you've given up and you've decided that you have no control over the outcome.

But the good news is that you can always change your outlook and when you do, it will change your destiny. Or if you already have a pretty good sense of ownership and accountability within your job, you can always continue to improve on it. Ask yourself each day how you can take more pride in your work, and how you can be more accountable to your employer and your team.

If you need some advice or further skill development to step up within your workplace, discuss your goals with your Human Resources professional or your manager, and let them know you are working on developing these particular leadership characteristics. Be open to their suggestions and follow through. Soon you will be on your way.

Become Highly Responsive and Direct

There is nothing worse than working on a deadline or an important project, and not hearing back from the people on the team. Imagine a manager who has sent emails or made calls but just doesn't hear back. It's almost impossible to navigate a decision through a workplace when there are delays at every turn because people are ignoring the person in charge.

If this sounds like you, I urge you not to continue to be *the roadblock*. Don't be the kind of person who dodges requests, causes more confusion, or the one with bad manners. Don't leave your team leader wondering if their message was received and don't send a vague or confusing reply because that will actually create more questions than it answers. Be clear and direct when you reply or you'll lose credibility among the leaders at your company and your peers. It is crazy-making if they have to come and chase you down for an answer; that will only lead to wasted energy and frustration.

Become someone with strong communication skills and who is highly responsive because then the people around you will know you can deliver results. Understand and accept that the people you work with need acknowledgement and they need their questions answered. Make it a point to always get back to people quickly with useful statements and clear input.

I know this is easier said than done, but if you truly want to excel at work, you need to develop habits that are responsive and direct. Manage your communications so that you don't get overwhelmed with the volume of messages that are exchanged. One good way to do this is to set some ground rules according to how you operate.

Here's an example. If there is a high priority project with looming deadlines, you'll want to flag those emails and answer them immediately. Tell others that you strive for a 24-hour turnaround. Another strategy is to get into the habit of replying to your emails at midday each day, and if you are swamped with a high priority project and an email concerns something that can wait, then send a reply like this: "I want to let you know that I've seen your email. I am currently working on another deadline and will be able to read this in full tomorrow. Please follow up with me the day after next and we can discuss it then."

Show That You are Intellectually Curious

People who get things done don't just take everything at face value. Instead they are intellectually curious and they always seem to be seeking *to know more*. They have a deep desire to learn about context and the broader landscape, so you'll find them asking questions like 'Who?' 'Why?' and 'How come?' They want to know if there is a good reason for doing something. *Is it the law?* Is it a leader's preference? Is it an old outdated system that makes us work this way? You get the idea.

Being intellectually curious equips these people to do a much better job. By asking questions, they understand who is networked, what the existing business relationships are, what motivates people, and many more interconnections within the world of work. As a result, they are better at connecting the dots, challenging the status quo, and delivering innovative thinking and solutions. In other words, intellectual curiosity lets them be highly resourceful and think outside of the box. Not surprisingly, people who deliver results are very often inquisitive about everything.

There have been many times that my curiosity has worked to my benefit. Here's one example. When I moved to a foreign country, I needed a driver's license. I was told that the usual process involved several weeks of on-road driving with an instructor, followed by a written test in a foreign language, a vision test, and a driving test.

At the time, I was juggling work and traveling across 14 countries. I needed to be able to deliver a positive impact immediately on the job, and establish relationships with my team and peers.

I didn't see how I could take hours out of my week for several months to study for a test in a foreign language and practice driving when I had a perfect driving record.

So the *intellectually curious* part of me asked myself: How come my existing driver's license was not recognized? I did a little research and learned that several US states and Canadian provinces had agreements in place so that their existing driving licenses would be recognized where I was living. However, there was no agreement with the province where I came from. So I placed a few phone calls and finally ended up speaking to someone who told me that it was a matter of paperwork and that it simply wasn't in place because no one had ever requested it before.

Aha, I thought so. There was a way to get this done, and from that point on, I was on a mission. It was actually pretty easy. I put in a formal written request to my government back home, and within a few short weeks, there was formal reciprocal driving agreement in place between my province and this country. *Voila!*

There have been many times in my life when I was able to find a way around something that seemed to me to be ridiculous. You can do the same. Be open to asking questions and challenging the status quo, without being totally annoying of course. Use your innate curiosity to see solutions and work-arounds that others may not see. Not every idea will work out, but most of the time it will – and you will be seen as someone who is not tied down to old methods and tired processes that just don't work in our modern world.

Learn How to Build Consensus

If you are going to deliver results by working with others, you have to know how to build consensus or agreement. The process of building consensus takes time, and once you understand how to do this well, it will serve you for a lifetime. It is well worth the investment of time upfront when you commit to building consensus because you can reduce barriers and hiccups later on.

Just to be clear, teams *work best* when you are able to identify the right people who need to contribute to your project, bring them together in a productive setting, and when you listen to their views. As someone able to build consensus among a group of people, you'll be the one who guides the conversation to ensure all perspectives are heard. That way you can identify everyone's goals, as well as their concerns. Get all of these on the table, clarify what you think you heard, and discuss options that everyone can live with.

You may have to repeat this process of going around the table, talking, listening and negotiating a few times in order to get everyone in agreement. It may also require that you be sensitive to different working styles and priorities. You may need to be a little dogged in your approach to ensure that you have inputs from key stakeholders who might be hard to track down or nail down. But when you take the time to build consensus, the results you deliver as a group will be all the more powerful because you secured greater buy-in, commitment, and understanding in the first place.

If you don't know how to build consensus, try to find a business leader in your company you can watch and learn from, or engage a coach who is highly skilled who can guide you in developing your abilities. Being able to build consensus comes with practice and maturity, but there is no time like the present to start watching others who do it well and to develop these skills for yourself.

Become a Strategic Listener

Listening is both an art and a skill, and it improves with practice. I like to think about this as strategic listening, and it is especially important when you are at work. I have found in my experience that too many people are focused only on their own agendas when they enter into discussions with peers, colleagues, management, or clients. They have their own points figured out and know exactly what they want to achieve, but they don't necessarily take enough time to listen to others. This is where conflict, misunderstanding, and division arise.

If you've ever been in a meeting with someone who just keeps nodding, and cutting people off by saying, yes, yes, yes, just so they can get out of there, you know what I mean. This can be so frustrating because you know they're not really listening, they're not taking a single note, and they're not seeking to really understand what's going on. And you can be pretty well assured that person is not invested in the topic at all and you'll get little if any follow-up from them.

When you are speaking with others in a business setting, you have to remain focused and present. You need to hear the words being said and also be mindful of the way the person is speaking, their body language, their emotional state, and what they might *not* be saying. Are they speaking through gritted teeth with a fake smile, saying they agree while clearly seething underneath? Are they constantly trying to change the subject and hijack the conversation to their own agenda? Are they distracted by their phone or the time or something else? Are you not at all sure what they are saying, even though they appear to be taking forever to make a point?

When you are focused and you sense something else might be afoot, or if something is not clear, make it a point to ask the right questions to clarify what is being said. Give the other person enough time to elaborate and make their opinion or objections clear. You can summarize what you've heard back to them, just to make sure you understand. If emotions appear to be running high, try to take a break to give things a chance to cool down and when you reconvene, try to find out what is underneath the deep feelings about the issue on the table.

The main thing is that you never want to leave a meeting or discussion with incomplete information. Instead of rushing through and rushing out, sit and take time to listen strategically and ask the right questions so you can get to the heart of the issue. I learned a lot of this in journalism school and have since practiced it every day in my career.

Strategic listening has helped me advance to new levels because I know how to ask the right questions and I strive to understand the full story. This came with practice and the fact that I always invest the time upfront in relationships to be sure I understand where the other person is coming from and how we can reach a middle ground. Listening well has allowed me to establish trust very effectively and efficiently, and that in turn has given me the capacity to consistently deliver results.

ESSENTIAL EXERCISE

ASK THE RIGHT QUESTIONS

Meetings can be fast-paced and everyone is busy. Listening well and asking the right questions are two ways you can stay on top of the content. Below are a number of questions that will help you to be sure that you fully understand any new assignments and you are clear on the details of a partnership or working relationship.

When you listen carefully, take notes, and ask the right questions, you will minimize disagreements, conflicts, or delays which can hinder your progress and impact overall profitability. Keep these questions handy and use them until you learn them by heart.

Ask the other person:
- What is your goal?
- How does it tie into the bigger strategy of the organization?
- How are you going to measure success? Do you have metrics?
- What's important to you personally on this project? Why?
- What barriers are you encountering?
- How are you addressing those barriers already, and is that working?
- How can I best be of assistance? Be specific.
- Who are you already working with?
- What timelines are you working under?
- What's going on in the broader landscape that helps or hinders progress with this work?
- Is there buy-in from the top? Is this project funded?
- What are the next steps after this work gets done?

Learn How to Paint a Vision and Sell Ideas

When you first find yourself in a position to pitch an idea, it's exciting. Congratulations! You have earned enough trust and respect to get time on the agenda. In order to make your voice heard, and to resonate with your audience, there are a number of details you'll want to pay attention to as you prepare for and deliver your big presentation.

As you are gathering your data, anticipate what the leaders of the group will need in order to move ahead with your ideas or recommendations. Don't make anyone have to ask for basic data. Do your homework in advance. In fact, *do more homework* than anyone else in the room. With the internet at your fingertips, there is no excuse not to come prepared, so look at the benchmarks, best practices, and current research in order to round out your ideas. Show them that you are thinking and make everyone in the room wish that you were on their team.

It is always a good idea to meet with your manager in advance, and any other important decision-makers, to get a sense of whether or not you have their support. If they have major concerns, try to deal with those in advance, or be prepared to speak to those concerns directly during your presentation.

Think through how the room will be set up for the meeting, what technology you need such as a microphone perhaps, and determine what kind of handouts you will distribute. Sometimes handouts work well but other times they can become a distraction or they might look like a waste of money. It's better to think these details through in advance. Always proofread any printed materials and electronic notes very carefully because spelling or grammar errors are other distractions you really don't need.

With regard to your content, be very clear what the problem statement is because that will be what frames your discussion. What are you trying to accomplish and why? What is wrong with the status quo and what specifically will be gained or solved if they adopt your approach? Include in your recommendation the expected timelines, what the key milestones will be, and the process of completion and ongoing maintenance.

Organize the Content of your Presentation

Personally, I like presentations where the recommendation is crystal clear and everyone can see it. I know that people always argue as to whether the recommendation should be stated upfront and followed up with the reasons why. To figure out if this is the right order in your case, think about the style of your organization and the culture of the place you are working in.

In some countries and industries, it is more common to state the decision or recommendation upfront. In other places or situations, the expectation is that you will present all the data first and build to a big ta-da moment. Just make sure you don't drag things out too long before you make your recommendation. Time is money and your audience may become impatient waiting for the *big reveal.*

When making your case, benchmarks are a good way to frame the discussion and help to give a broader perspective. This includes things like what other companies are doing in the industry. If there are any official bodies that report and compile indices, surveys, or best practices, then use these strategically.

The same thing is true with historical trends; if you have past data, be sure to show it. Multi-year data is very important, especially in cases where you are talking about the financial requirements. To find out what you can access, ask more experienced colleagues what financial data is available and appropriate for you to use.

If you are asking for specific resources to be employed, be sure to include not only the dollars to be invested but also any partners who need to support the effort and which key employees might need to be reassigned to make it work. Be clear about the time commitments you are asking for because no doubt those existing employees are already busy with competing priorities.

Whenever you are making a formal presentation, understand that there will be a number of essential elements needed for success. I call these *key success factors*. For example, you may need to secure employee buy-in and you might need a project manager so that all deadlines are met in the right order. There may be constant need to have your databases updated and that will take extra resources. You might be looking at landing new key clients and if so, you'll need to spend time and money to accomplish that. Add up the costs of gathering testimonials, presenting at a special showcase conference for your industry, or landing strategic media interviews with top reporters or influencers in your markets.

In your presentation, give an objective assessment of what happens if we do *this* versus *that*. What is the cost of moving forward as compared to staying with the status quo? Always show a choice, and that you've thought about compromises. Using language like *return on investment* is good, but don't overstate things or exaggerate. Just keep to the facts. I often find it's best to distance yourself from the decision. Remember, it's not about you or your team. It's about the greater good of the organization.

❖

ESSENTIAL EXERCISE

LINE UP YOUR SUPPORTERS

If you have a major initiative that you are championing, or if you are on a team that is doing this, then take some time to list all the key people you will have to involve and what their likely positions or opinions will be. Think about the decision-makers and anticipate what stance they are likely to take on the matter. When you gather these details in advance of your major presentation, you can react in *real time* during the meeting, rather than being caught off-guard by objections that you weren't expecting. Here are some techniques for you to consider:

- In order to understand the important opinions, try conducting a series of informal survey interviews with your key stakeholders related to the project in order to determine where they stand and what their most important concerns or questions are. Listen strategically and take notes so you can be prepared to address any important objections in your presentation.

- You can also look at their track-record to see what initiatives these influencers or leaders have supported in the past and why. That will give you an idea if they will likely support your recommendations or not.

- Find out if there are any hot-buttons about this topic or initiative that have been stumbling blocks in the past. You may have to use your intellectual curiosity to work around these blocks or to get rid of them, before you'll be able to proceed with your ideas.

Essential Exercise

Get Recognized for the Results you Achieve

As you begin to gain a reputation for delivering results, find ways to stay top of mind with your team, your manager, and the key decision-makers and influencers you need to impress. Here is a summary of some techniques you can use.

- Take the initiative to book a meeting with your manager to highlight strategic steps you've taken and to demonstrate measureable results in your current projects.
- Remember to talk about your successes at regular monthly and quarterly meetings.
- Select a new assignment you've been given and break down the work into key milestones to create a series of wins for yourself.
- Choose a hot topic in your workplace and use your creativity and intellectual curiosity to explore various angles and potential solutions. Bring your ideas forward in the next meeting with your manager.
- Research industry awards programs that you or your team can apply for to get outside recognition.

The next chapter takes you to the next level through embracing risk for career growth. But not all risks are worth taking. Learn how to assess risks to see if they are right for you, and understand how calculated risk taking will improve your confidence, skills, networks, and how others see you. It can be a game-changer.

KEY POINTS FROM CHAPTER 8

- Demonstrate accountability by always following up when you say you will and do what you promise to do.
- Be highly responsive and direct to keep work flowing and decisions moving along.
- Reveal new options and solutions by asking the right questions. When you hit a wall, be resourceful. Use your intellectual curiosity to break through any blocks or barriers.
- Learn how to build consensus and work effectively with others.
- Become a strategic listener. Ask the right questions and understand where people are truly coming from.
- Manage key stakeholders and line up your supporters in advance of any major pitches.
- Link your results to the big picture. Connect the dots and add value to the strategy.

CHAPTER 9

TAKE CALCULATED RISK

Everyone has a different risk tolerance because some people just don't like uncertainty, unpredictability, or uncontrollable circumstances. But regardless of the fact that uncertainty exists, *action still needs to be taken.* The reason it can be upsetting to move forward is that there is the potential of gaining or losing something of value. Think about your own risk tolerance and under what circumstances you might be willing to take a risk.

The degree of risk depends on a number of factors, but overall we can say that there are generally four types of risk: physical safety; financial risk; social standing; and emotional risk. I find it interesting how people react to these various kinds of risks. For example, some people will jump out of planes, but won't ever confront a difficult family member. Others will risk their fortune for the thrill of gambling but would never use their voice to protest something in society where they could potentially lose standing within their social circle.

In order to get a handle on this topic, it's best to start by acknowledging that life is full of risks and we can't avoid that. We take risks when we choose a major in school, when we change jobs, when we get married, when we start a family, and when we make investments. I expect that you took some risks today already and you probably do every day, so pat yourself on the back. You've already learned a lot from just living your life, and you're still doing just fine.

The Value of Becoming a Good Risk Taker

You already know that you have to take some risks if you want to achieve your dreams and live life to the fullest. It's what helps you grow and become a stronger, more experienced individual. It gives you confidence and creates more opportunities. Risk is essential if you are to achieve anything you desire.

As an adult proceeding through life, even simple things can feel risky. They did for me and I bet they do for you. For example, it can feel like a risk to stay in to work on a project while all of your friends are out at a club. This is the risk of *missing out*. I did this a lot when I started to build my corporate career and I worked nights to establish a real estate business on the side.

You may also be fearful of losing friendships, but in reality sometimes our friends actually hold us back. As we grow, we begin to develop different interests and goals. Rest assured that true friends will recognize that you need to spread your wings sometimes. For example, I am currently mentoring an MBA student who really wanted to take a work-term abroad to get experience in Europe for a semester. Her friends however were telling her how much she'd miss back at home, such as the fun times, boyfriends, getting an apartment together, and starting work together.

Those friends almost had her convinced to stay, but I talked to her about pros and cons, the bigger picture, and how sometimes we need to sacrifice more beer nights to build a solid future and realize dreams in the long term. She took all the feedback into consideration and she has decided to leave this spring for a semester abroad. This is a good example of how she sought out trusted advisors, listened to her gut, and believed in herself.

The other risk for early career starters is the risk of looking silly, being judged, and admitting we don't know something. This is a very real concern because there is a risk whenever you put yourself out there and you can sometimes be vulnerable in a work setting. It's healthy to ask questions and wonder about things, so I encourage you to do that, but also know that you are far more capable than you feel inside. This is true of everyone, so practice taking calculated risks as often as you can. The more you do it, the less chance that you will get into the kind of rut where you always seem to feel stuck or paralyzed by fear.

In this chapter, I'm going to give you a totally doable and practical approach to assessing risk and managing fear in your life. This is such an incredibly important skill. I found that it made a world of difference to me that I was able to figure this out at a relatively young age. You can do it too and here's how.

What is Calculated Risk Taking?

Calculated risk taking is a chance that you take after careful estimation of the probable outcome. Approaching risk in this way will bring significant benefits to your life and to your career, but it also comes with some barriers that you may have to overcome. Let's look at the benefits first.

Whenever you take a risk, it can help you stand out from peers, plus it shows that you have confidence and are committed to growth. You tend to learn a lot about yourself from taking risks. You also gain new experiences and new transferable skills, while others are not learning because they are sitting still.

Since you're moving forward, you'll also discover new networks and other aspects of your chosen career path you never thought about before. In the short run and long run, you'll achieve more of your dreams. And for the things that may not work out the first time, you'll pick up helpful coping mechanisms to enable you to bounce back when you make mistakes. Even better, you'll no longer have to worry about the fear of failure or wonder about the road not taken. That is a hugely liberating feeling.

But of course, along with these substantial benefits, there are barriers. A number of things can stop us from taking calculated risks and achieving more of our dreams. As humans, we have a natural tendency to try to stay safe and avoid change or failure. Almost everyone fears failure, making mistakes, rejection, or judgment so any one of those things can hold us back. Whenever we lack confidence or are unwilling to be flexible, that can keep us from taking risks.

We may fear we won't be safe if we move out of our comfort zone. Or we may feel unable to take a risk because we just don't have a clear vision for ourselves or a life plan. In other cases, we may not have any support or encouragement from family and friends, or they can sometimes hold us back because they are scared or jealous. Without a mentor, role model, or any supporters, taking a risk can sometimes seem just too scary, thus we keep our feet firmly planted and don't move beyond our usual parameters.

Fortunately, none of these barriers are insurmountable. I believe that knowledge is power and I'm happy to share with you a powerful approach to assessing risk and overcoming any barriers in your way. But first, let's see what your aptitude is right now for taking risks.

ESSENTIAL EXERCISE

TEST YOUR APTITUDE AS A CALCULATED RISK TAKER

We all experience barriers to taking risks at times, and as I mentioned, I will give you a methodology to push through. But just before doing that, I encourage you to try this exercise to see what your aptitude is for taking risk. It's a quick test that will give you some food for thought as we move through the rest of this chapter.

Below are what I call the *Top 10 Attributes of a Calculated Risk Taker*. Give yourself a score on a scale of 1 to 5 to see how you fare. Perhaps you've never even thought of yourself in this way before, so just the fact that you are thinking about risk in a new way is progress. I believe these skills below are ones that you can cultivate with experience, and over time, all you need is to practice and have a willingness to fail and learn.

Think about your current abilities as they relate to risk and rank each statement below from 1 to 5 (one being the lowest, something you're not at all good at – and five being the highest, something that you feel confident about and at which you excel):

1 Being able to act on incomplete information.
Your ranking: _____

2 Good at judging situations in time to act appropriately.
Your ranking: _____

3 Being self-aware, with the ability to accurately assess your own limitations and capabilities.
Your ranking: _____

4 Understanding the skills and knowledge required in any given situation to succeed, and being prepared to close any gaps.
Your ranking: _____

5 Being good at evaluating the benefits and costs of a risk.
Your ranking: _____

6 Setting challenging and attainable goals.
Your ranking: _____

7 Being able to accept failure.
Your ranking: _____

8 Using information to calculate the likelihood of success.
Your ranking: _____

9 Being resourceful and understanding how to navigate people and processes.
Your ranking: _____

10 Understanding stress triggers and how to overcome them.
Your ranking: _____

Whether you scored yourself low or high, you now know where you stand. And it is critically important to understand that whenever opportunities surface in life that appear to have inherent risk, you will need to be able to effectively – and objectively – evaluate them. That's what's coming up next, the framework you need to make this happen.

ESSENTIAL EXERCISE

APPLY THE CRAWL METHOD

I have learned this method through trial and error and I refer to it as *The CRAWL Method* of dealing with risk. While I've always taken career risk, I haven't always been good at it and I didn't always have this method at my fingertips. This is something that I figured out over time and I now share it widely because it has proven so valuable.

So what is CRAWL exactly? It's an acronym for an easy-to-remember and effective process for logically thinking through risk. The C & R stand for *Calculated Risk*. The A is for *Analysis of the Situation*. The W is for *Worst-case Scenario* and L stands for the *Likelihood of Success*. When you apply this approach, you can much more clearly see what you have to gain or lose if you proceed with a certain action or not.

When faced with a decision that seems to have some risk, the first step is actually to recognize that this would be a good time to apply *The CRAWL Method*. Basically, it acts as a reminder for you to slow down and think through things before you leap in, and then it gives you a way to evaluate the opportunity or risk in an objective and unhurried way.

So when would you apply the CRAWL steps? You can use them any time that you face a job move where you have to assume significant more responsibility or whenever you are facing or considering a relocation. It can be very helpful whenever you think about enrolling in some more formal education that will compete for your time. You may also use CRAWL if you are being offered the chance to take on volunteer duties in your community or in your industry which may put you in the spotlight or the line of fire.

At this point, I will run through the CRAWL steps and explain each one. Then you can read through a couple of real life examples and better understand how this works. After that, I encourage you to try the *Essential Exercise* at the end of this chapter as the template for your own risk analysis and decision-making.

1 *"C-R" stands for Calculated Risk.* Your first step is to identify the *calculated risk.* Write it down. Think about all of the associated risks that would go with that action. For example, if your *calculated risk* is to take a new job you don't have experience doing, it's clear that you will be assuming some kind of risk that you might not like this job, you might not be good at it, and if you are lousy at it, that could impact your career trajectory. It's important to also consider that this action might impact your finances, and may even eat into your family time or personal time. So be sure to consider all of the aspects of the risk that you can think of.

2 *"A" stands for Analysis of the Situation.* When you analyze the situation, follow this five-step process. It helps if you talk this through with someone you trust to ensure you are seeing it from a number of angles.

1. List the pros – the positive things that will come from this action.
2. List the cons – the negative things that will come from this action.
3. List the unknowns about taking this action.
4. Ask yourself if you can live with the cons.
5. Ask yourself if you can turn any of the cons into pros? How? Be specific because this will feed into your Action Plan should you proceed with taking the risk.

3 *"W" stands for Worst-case Scenario.* Write down the absolute worst-case scenario that could happen. Now, ask yourself if you can live with it, and what you would do if it happens. Write it out.

4 *"L" stands for Likelihood of Success.* For this last step, you have to know yourself very well. You also have to be prepared to be realistic and brutally honest. Taking everything into consideration, do you think you'll be successful? Do you have the skills, experience, inner fortitude, resourcefulness, and networks to help you succeed? If your answer is yes, you quite likely have what it takes to proceed forward and embrace the risk.

But if your answer is no, don't quit yet. Ask yourself: Are there certain parts of the opportunity that you are comfortable with, but perhaps other aspects that you are not? Maybe you can negotiate certain parts in or out, depending on what would suit you better. The following real life lesson is a case in point where a person I know used her intellectual curiosity and negotiating skills to make an unfavorable risk into a much more palatable one.

Real Life Lesson

Using Negotiation to Mitigate Risk

I once had a call from an individual whom I was mentoring who got a job offer from his dream company, but they were offering significantly less money than he wanted to accept. He wasn't sure what to do. He really wanted to work for this company since it was an industry leader that was admired around the world.

He knew the company could provide him with a more professional work experience, a boost to his resume credentials, and a greatly expanded network. He liked all of those aspects of the offer. But he had a lot of student debt and really couldn't afford to take a cut in pay.

At the same time, he had an offer from another company for much more money than he was currently making, but it wasn't a company that was even in his top five choices of companies to work for. It had no reputation to speak of, and was more of a boutique firm than a global corporation. It would have limited opportunities for advancement for him.

Together we discussed a strategy that he could take but it came with risk. He could approach the preferred company with his own counter-offer. He could say: "Thanks, but I will have to decline the offer as it stands. I've always dreamed of working for you, and I believe I could bring tremendous value and hit the ground running immediately, but I've got a competing offer for X amount more money. If you are able to match it, I'll come to you. If not, I'm sorry, but I'll have to take the other offer. I value my skills and I believe in my market value too much to lower my earnings at this point."

We took about 30 minutes and talked through this action using *The CRAWL Method*. The worst-case scenario was that they would say no to the additional money, and then he would have to take the other offer with the firm he didn't like as much. Or he could go back to the global leader and accept their original offer of a lesser amount of money (which was really not feasible for him financially), and ultimately compromise his credibility.

He slept on it and determined that he could live with the worst-case scenario. He went for it and *guess what*? He got the job at the better company, and secured the increased wage level that he wanted to get!

So you see, you can always say no to a risky action, but before you do, really think about ways you might bring down the level of risk to something you can live with. It's a great way to make sure you don't shortchange yourself over an opportunity that could be the perfect match for you, with just a little bit of creativity, negotiation, and calculated risk.

REAL LIFE LESSON

CALCULATED RISK TAKING FOR CAREER GROWTH

Sarah was an executive for a regional pharmaceutical company. She had joined the organization right out of university and made her way up through the management ranks quickly. She had been there for just over 10 years, and had been in the role of Vice President of Communications for half of that time. She led a large team, enjoyed a strong reputation, and was very confident and comfortable in her role.

But things were not so rosy in the overall industry. Mergers and consolidations seemed to be in the business news just about every day. Sarah's boss kept suggesting that she should think about relocating to the city where he worked in order to be closer to him and so that she could be more visible to the other senior decision-makers.

Sarah kept resisting the idea of a move. She didn't logically see why she needed to relocate. Nothing was falling through the cracks in her view and she wasn't incurring excessive travel costs. Plus, what if her current boss suddenly left and she found herself reporting to someone else in another city, and she'd have to move yet again, all for the same job? She had seen that happen with a few of her colleagues who were being bounced around all over the place.

She and her husband were in their early 30s and the talk of all the industry upheaval and a potential move made Sarah's heart drop. It was a terrible idea for her family life because they had just renovated their dream home and were thinking of starting a family. On top of that, Sarah knew that her husband loved his current job that was nearby where they lived and together they were building a side business that needed their attention.

One day, a call came out of the blue from a former boss offering Sarah a job in another country. It was in a similar industry, but not exactly the same. It was at a vice president level and she would be responsible for two functions: Communications which she knew extremely well, and Human Resources for which she didn't have any previous responsibility.

As she researched the new opportunity, she learned that the primary challenges were on the labor front because the company operated within a highly unionized environment. A recession had hit and there would be immediate changes that she would need to lead upon her arrival. To complicate matters, the role would oversee HR strategy for 14 counties, all with different employee legislation in various languages and many different kinds of cultural concerns.

On the surface, the move was lateral in level and title. But there were greater functional responsibilities, broader scope, and increased complexity given the geographical reach. There would be a huge learning curve because it was a new industry to her, and the company stated they wanted her to earn her global credentials in HR within the first year.

With regard to compensation, it looked on the surface to be about the same, but there were some caveats. The executive bonus, which was an attractive part of the overall compensation package, had not paid out in recent years. In terms of base pay, there was a pay freeze in place given the recession, so she was warned not to expect any significant increases in the foreseeable future.

Even though she was being hired to work in another country, she was not being offered any expatriate expenses or relocation costs. She would have to foot the housing bill herself, which was three to four times the cost of housing she was paying at home, and of course she would face the usual one-time costs associated with purchases to set up a new home.

The company agreed to pay for travel to the new country in order to start the job, but any travel back and forth to home after that would have to be at her own expense. The company would handle all immigration costs related to visa paperwork, and they would also pay for a car and fuel. Sarah's mind was spinning with excitement, but also a good deal of apprehension as she pulled out her pen and started to analyze the situation using *The CRAWL Method*. Her notes went like this.

Analysis of the Situation – 1) The PROS: Career growth, international expansion, diversifying to a new industry, embracing a change before one might be forced upon her, maintaining an executive role, future growth potential with a global leader, and she had the confidence of the CEO.

Analysis of the Situation – 2) The CONS: Leaving a familiar job for one she was untested in, no track record in those parts of the world, no network to rely on, she would have to rebuild her reputation and credibility, huge expectations for immediate impact (could she deliver?), language barriers, impact on family, the company wanted her to take personality and IQ tests to assess her suitability, and of course, there were the financial costs of the move that she would have to bear.

Analysis of the Situation – 3) The Unknowns: Pay variability, currency, housing, tax treatments, visas and immigration paperwork, bank accounts, driver's license, personal security, and medical care. Could her husband secure suitable work? Would it be practical to start a family there without extended family close by and not knowing what kind of medical coverage would be available? The list of "unknowns" seemed to be overwhelming.

Analysis of the Situation – 4) Can she live with the cons and the unknowns? She felt in her heart the answer was yes, but from a practical perspective, Sarah found that she couldn't make a final decision until she did quite a bit more homework. Many calls later with the company, tax and immigration advisors, and discussions with her family allowed her to answer almost all of the unknowns to the best extent possible and almost all were in her favor. Yes, she decided that she could live with the cons and some uncertainty.

Analysis of the Situation – 5) Could she turn any cons into pros?
Maybe she could make family visits from her parents and in-laws
into opportunities to tour a new part of the world together.
Perhaps she could establish new networks for later in life. The
new certifications would really add to her credentials, provided
she could manage the stress of studying while also learning
the ropes at the new company. She knew French well, and a bit
of Spanish already, so she felt the language proficiency could
be managed by brushing up and would be enhanced greatly
by immersion.

Worst-case Scenario: The worst-case scenario she could think of
was failure. They might hate her. She might have to return home
with no job because she would have left a really good job in the
midst of industry change. She would lose the money and time
that had been invested in making the move abroad. Her reputation could take a hit back home when it became known that she
couldn't make it work overseas.

What did she decide? The analysis showed that she could make
it work from a practical perspective, but at the end of the day,
Sarah found she had to look inward. Did she have the
motivation, fortitude, and resourcefulness to handle this kind
of significant change and challenge? Would her track record of
strong performance and intellectual curiosity be enough for her
to succeed in a whole new world? *Did she believe she would succeed?*
Yes, the answer was definitely yes.

Sarah accepted the move and put in place a rigorous life plan that would stack the odds in her favor. Three of the most important elements of that life plan included: strict timelines to establish new networks; creating a series of milestones for "quick wins" that would demonstrate her positive impact almost immediately; and she negotiated specific time off in short spurts so she could focus on studying for and securing the necessary HR certifications that were expected.

After Sarah took the leap of faith and the new job, there were a number of surprises that she and her family faced, both good and bad. With regard to personal relationships, she and her husband were very good at trust and were committed to helping each other follow their dreams. They decided he would stay behind just in case things didn't work out overseas. He kept his job, kept their side business going, and they were able to keep their dream home.

As a couple, they commuted and met as often as they could for weekend visits, and they adjusted their schedules to make sure they stayed connected and Skyped every day. But Sarah found that isolation was a bigger issue than she had thought it would be. It was not easy to go places where she had no connections or friends. She did forge a few close contacts with colleagues but didn't have much time for socializing outside of work. It turned out to be a crazy, busy time just learning the job and the world of pharmaceuticals while travelling so much within that role.

The learning curve was so much more than she could have ever imagined, but then again nothing could ever replace the experience of immersing herself in a foreign country. She learned how to accelerate trust and credibility within a whole new industry and culture.

The tax realities and immigration matters however seemed to be a moving target. She would think she had it figured out, but there always seemed to be some surprise change to government policies, treaties, or tax laws that caught her off guard. It was an ongoing headache and one of the uncertainties that she just had to learn to live with. But on the other hand, she did learn a lot about international economic realities.

When they look back on that period of time, Sarah and her husband agree that the rewards outweighed the risks and they don't regret the five years that Sarah worked abroad. They got to see places for the first time and enjoy a ton of travel together and she was able to increase her confidence and credentials as a global professional. And fortunately, there was still time to start a family which they did the year after she returned from overseas.

ESSENTIAL EXERCISE

DO YOUR OWN RISK ASSESSMENT USING CRAWL

Choose a scenario you are grappling with right now in your personal or professional life. Select something that you have been dreaming about or weighing in terms of taking a risk and that you would like some clarity on. Use *The CRAWL Method* to begin to sort it out.

C-R – Calculated Risk: First identify the calculated risk and then think about all of the associated risks that would go along with it. Write this all down so it is clear.

A – Analyze the Situation: Work through each part of the following five-step process and make note of what comes to mind or what you find out through your research.
1. List the pros.
2. List the cons.
3. List the unknowns.
4. Ask yourself if you can live with the cons.
5. Ask yourself if you can turn any of the cons into pros? How?

W – Worst-case Scenario: Write down the absolute worst-case scenario that could happen.

L – Likelihood of Success: Taking everything into consideration, do you think you will be successful? If the answer is yes, then work out the steps you need in order to begin to take action.

The next chapter looks into life beyond work. The higher you rise, the more life will throw at you. Distractions can add pressure if not properly managed. Managing how you spend your time, and understanding your physical, mental, and spiritual needs will help keep you in top form and motivated to be your best.

KEY POINTS FROM CHAPTER 9

- If you're comfortable, you are not growing. You will only grow by taking some risks.
- Keep reminding yourself of your dreams and your plans, and seek out appropriate challenges.
- Use *The CRAWL Method* to fully assess the risk you are contemplating.
- Making a chart of pros versus cons is a great decision-making tool.
- Any time you are about to embrace a significant change, be realistic about your likelihood of success.
- Accept the fact that failure is OK.

Chapter 10

Find the Ideal Work-Life Balance for You

If you could bottle up a magic elixir called *work-life balance*, you could retire right now. Everyone wants it but is there really such a thing? This phrase has been thrown around for a long time now, but I say it's time to dispel the myth. Work-life balance is an outdated concept that implies two very backward and unattainable goals. Let me explain.

First, the term work-life balance implies that you need to compartmentalize your life in two distinct parts: work and life. It leaves the impression that somehow, we need to balance or offset our work identity and obligations with the entirety of the rest of our life. That would mean that I would place my job title "author, expert and speaker" on one side of the page, and the rest of my life goes on the other, which would read: "daughter, wife, mother, volunteer, community activist, healthy and fiercely formidable change agent for world peace." You get the idea.

Surely this is faulty logic because you cannot look at "work" and "everything else" as *equal parts*. Work is just one component of your entire life. It's an extremely important component because it fills a lot of your waking hours and it provides the wage that you need to live comfortably, support yourself and your family, and pursue your dreams, but it still remains just one part. I encourage you to keep that in perspective.

Second, the term work-life balance gives *work* a bad name. It implies that somehow work is something we must trudge through so that we can enjoy the rest of our life. I don't believe work should get shortchanged or mislabeled. Work can and should be a very fulfilling part of life that we look forward to and enjoy. In fact, if you want to live a more fulfilled life, then one of the best ways is to develop a healthier relationship with your career.

Some companies have started to call this concept *Work-life Effectiveness* which removes the "balance" part of things, but this still implies there is an inherent separation between work and all other aspects of life. But as I say, this just isn't true. Work and life are completely intertwined, both because of societal demands and because of our own human need to be connected to everything all the time. Of course we find that technology reinforces this integration.

Lots of people juggle everyday life events and tasks into their work schedule – any parent will confirm that. You'll find that friends and co-workers openly discuss their competing priorities and we all try to squeeze life tasks into our workday hours if we can because we are so crunched for time.

Most companies now accept that time at work will naturally involve some distractions caused by our lives outside of work. Progressive companies even offer considerable flexibility in order to meet family obligations and thus the growth of flex programs like telecommuting, job sharing, compressed work weeks, and more. But these remain by far the exception, not the rule.

Other stress-busting initiatives in workplaces are driven by a focus on physical wellness, such as onsite yoga, ergonomic assessments for office workers, healthy eating challenges, free salads on Fridays, and the like.

Still many employers expect their employees to check and reply to texts or emails while "off the clock". This is a reality that is not likely to change so it's up to you to find a balance so that work tasks don't completely take over your whole life 24/7. To their credit, some employers are recognizing this as a problem and attempting to cut back on disturbing employees while they are not at work. But it's not the rule yet, and no matter how flexible or progressive your workplace is, your employer is not the one who controls the quality of your life. That responsibility rests solely with you: only you can control how you juggle things and find fulfillment in your days.

Work Smarter, Not Harder

If you want to consistently have good days at work and at home, it starts with thinking differently about the outdated concepts of work-life balance. I encourage you to think about taking charge. You need to reclaim the way you conduct yourself at work and how you take care of your overall health which involves your mind, body, and spirit. This chapter covers a range of practical techniques and perspectives to help you do just that.

Since work is such a large part of your waking day, try to ensure that you run your day, instead of having the day *run you*. And as I mentioned earlier, while employers can do things to introduce more flexibility, hire better leaders and offer perks, in the end, it's your responsibility. You have the biggest influence over how your day unfolds and what you achieve.

The good news is that there is a lot you can do to make sure you accomplish what you need to and leave work satisfied with your contribution at the end of the day. I often suggest that a great starting point is to master the art of time management.

You may already do this well, but a refresher is never a bad thing. Or if you are someone who is consistently behind on your deliverables, late for meetings, or wondering where did the day go, then these next five key skills can change your life. Specifically, I encourage you to:

- Set realistic goals.
- Prioritize your time.
- Scope your work out properly.
- Create a personal organizational strategy.
- Learn to manage disruptions.

Set Realistic Goals

I mentioned SMART goal setting before and now I'd like to dig in and explain it in more detail. Once you determine what work goals or personal goals you need and want to accomplish in any given month or week, the SMART goal setting system will help you make them more tangible.

SMART goals refer to goals that are specific, measureable, attainable, relevant, and time bound. A lot of people and teams talk about *what needs to get done* to improve outcomes, but somehow they just never get it done. These people and teams are weak at execution. They don't follow up with the simple steps that are needed to actually achieve the goal. Instead they linger, time passes, pressure builds, frustration mounts, and panic sets in. But you can avoid all of that by setting realistic goals that are actually achievable given your environment, and managing everyone's expectations around when and how they are going to be achieved.

For example, say you are a sales manager and you've gotten feedback that you need to establish new relationships with potential clients in the medical field. You've heard about growth in that sector and want to establish a network and begin to sell into that new market. You can set a SMART goal that reads like this: "I will establish 10 new contacts in the medical field we are trying to sell into, and I will secure three meetings with potential clients in the coming two months." This works because it meets the five criteria of SMART goals: specific, measurable, attainable, relevant, and time bound.

First, it is specific. You'll know if you succeeded or not. Then it is also measurable because you have set the quantity of contacts and the number of meetings. It's attainable because the number is not overwhelming. In eight weeks, you should be able to establish 10 new contacts and have three of them agree to meetings. It's relevant because it is linked to your sales targets and the company's strategy. Plus it is time bound, and it's also good that the time horizon is two months which is fairly near term, rather than being too far off in time.

Prioritize your Time

Even if all the goals you set are SMART, they are not all created equal. You can think of yourself as a running coach, guiding all of the various goals and ushering them toward the finish line with everyone high-fiving at the end of the race. *How do you do this?* Take all goals in any given period (year, quarter, month, and week) and prioritize them.

To do this, step back and look at the impact of each goal. Which ones are most important for the health and competitiveness of your organization? Are there some that will benefit you and the organization more so than others? Take into consideration your environment and the broader strategy of your organization. Create your list of priority goals for the given time period (month, quarter, and so on) and then review them with your manager.

Now look at things that are deadline dependent, resource dependent, and interlinked. This will help you sequence your goals to make sure that you are getting the necessary inputs from others in time to achieve your goals.

Then I like to suggest that you set some false deadlines or early deadlines for yourself and others. This will help you manage the flow of your work carefully and avoid crunch mode when everyone is stressed out. So if you know something has to be done for April 1, say to your team that the deadline is March 15, which gives you two weeks in case anything major happens. When you build in a buffer, no one will be in panic mode on March 31. Prioritizing work significantly increases your likelihood of getting things done properly and getting each of them crossed off your list.

REAL LIFE LESSON

SCOPING WORK OUT PROPERLY

Scoping out a work project means becoming really clear on what is needed and by when. Often people will take on an assignment with a nod of a head, and walk away not fully understanding what is being requested. Perhaps you can identify with the following interaction between Joe and his manager and realize how important scope is when you want to be efficient.

Manager: "Joe, can you come see me for a minute please? I have something important I need you to work on."

Joe: "Sure. I'll be right there." Joe rushes up from his desk and pops into the manager's office. No pen or paper in hand, just himself.

Manager: "Joe, we have a big client meeting next week. I want some trends run on how much money we've earned from this client in the last five years. You know ... what kind of business have they been giving us. OK? I need it on my desk by Wednesday morning. The meeting is noon that day with the client."

Joe leaves. It's Thursday. He has access to reports and he figures that he can get working on this the next day. But Friday comes and goes. Joe had some other work he wanted to finish up, and his co-workers kept dropping by with interruptions. He had planned to leave early to head off for a weekend getaway with his friends. He didn't get anything started on the manager's request as he heads into the weekend. Monday arrives after a restful weekend and he sees his manager in the parking lot.

Manager: "Morning Joe. Good weekend?"

Joe: "Yes, it was great. You?"

Manager: "Yup. Listen, we have a busy week ahead of us. We're trying to meet with some key clients and understand how we can grow those accounts. I know I asked for you to get me some numbers for Wednesday morning, but if you could, I'd like it Tuesday at 5 p.m. so I can take it home to think about it. I realize I need more time to prep. The boss has booked me for a briefing Wednesday morning so he can be ready as we move into the meetings, so that means I'm crunched for time. No pressure, but I would sure appreciate it if I could see something Tuesday before I go home."

Joe: "OK. I'll do my best."

Joe sits down at his desk trying to remember what they discussed last Thursday. Did his manager want revenue trends for five years or profit? Did he want a breakdown of the type of business the client bought, or was it more about the frequency and volume? Joe didn't take any notes, and since he left it until Monday, his memory was a little foggy. He was starting to feel overwhelmed and embarrassed that he didn't fully listen or ask the right questions. He popped by his manager's office to clarify it but the manager had left for some outside meetings and would not be back until the next day.

Joe returned to his desk and started to pull some data. He pulled everything he could find, and leaned on co-workers to stop what they were doing to help him develop graphs and charts. He spent all night designing an elaborate presentation with five-year trends on every key metric. Any aspect of the business he could think of, he included. He delivered the report Tuesday afternoon by email so he knew his boss would have it to review that evening. It was 20 pages long.

The next day he saw his manager in the parking lot on his way home for the day.

Joe: "Hi. Did you get the report I did? How did the meeting go?"

Manager: "Yes, I got it but I wasn't able to read it all the way through, it was just too long. I was really just looking for revenue growth over the last five years, not a 20-page report. But I appreciate it. Not to worry. Maybe we'll do a deeper dive into this customer and review all of the data and metrics you assembled. I'm really focused just at the highest level right now."

Joe felt deflated. All of his hard work seemed to go unnoticed, and he had now fallen behind on other requests and deadlines. This wasn't the first time he felt this way, and he couldn't shake the sense that his boss was ungrateful or unappreciative. And a poor communicator.

The fact is that it was Joe who was the poor communicator. He didn't listen or take notes. He didn't ask any relevant questions about the scope of the assignment. He had an opportunity the very first time it was mentioned to write down specific details and understand exactly what his manager wanted and why. Instead, because he had no written record of the conversation, he lost a ton of extra time. He didn't work out the scope properly and he over-delivered to the point that the information was way too detailed and not useful for its purpose.

ESSENTIAL EXERCISE

CREATE A PERSONAL ORGANIZATIONAL STRATEGY

The process of staying organized and getting things done is a pretty personal thing. We all have our own systems and preferences on how we keep track of our tasks and goals. Some of us are obsessive, writing lists upon lists of activities multiple times a day, others set our alarms on our phones to remind us of meetings or deadlines. Some people use memory tricks to associate words and concepts, and trigger mental reminders. Whatever your style, you must find an organizational strategy that works for you, that you are committed to maintaining, and that actually delivers results.

A system is important – whether it's electronic on your handheld, or a daily journal. Keep a system where your time is logged, your actions captured, and your notes can be tracked and recorded. This system will help you stay organized and focused, and it will be handy to reference when it comes time for performance reviews.

When selecting an organizational system, find one that has these six components within it.

1 *A detailed calendar.* Learn to think about time in terms of 'chunks' – annual strategies, monthly goals, weekly objectives, and daily to-dos. These must be handy so you can reference them at any time. If you are just looking at a weekly view, but not able to quickly compare it against your quarterly or monthly priorities, then it won't serve you as well.

2 *An agenda with specific time allocations.* Look for an agenda system with time broken down to 30-minute increments. It's better to have a process that encourages you to get a ton done in 30 minutes so you're far less likely to waste time frivolously chatting with a co-worker. If you don't plan carefully and use your time wisely, time will evaporate.

3 *To-do lists are important.* A good to-do list means you can put your goals into actions and the list will guide how you spend your time. Start fresh every day by revisiting old to-do lists and creating a new one. This way you'll stay current, organized, and focused. Plus, you'll feel good about everything you achieved yesterday, and feel motivated to make a big impact again today.

4 *Take notes.* Taking notes is the best way to properly capture the contents of a discussion and decision points. So make sure your system has a place for notes that are relevant to any of your to-do tasks, points discussed in meetings, directives, and so on. If you are using an electronic system, attachments work well. If you are using a paper system, find one that allows you to insert notes next to the relevant day. I have found myself revisiting notes regularly for legal inquiries or to provide an objective perspective to company leaders on the particulars of a question being discussed.

5 *Build in time to think.* Avoid overscheduling every minute of the day. You need time to breathe and collect your thoughts, rehearse your points, replay what you just learned, or read material so you can fully digest it.

6 *Make your meetings work for you.* Don't spend your day in meetings that are unfocused, with no agenda, and too many people who really don't need to be there (including you). Understand why you are being asked to attend a meeting. Cluster items and combine two or more things in a meeting with a single person whenever you can. Don't book one hour with your manager to talk about just one topic. Be efficient, get in and get out, so you can get on with your work and deliver results.

Learn to Manage Disruptions

If you really want to make the most effective use of your time, learn to manage disruptions like a pro. There will constantly be disruptions in the workplace, and the higher you rise in your career, the more distractions there will be. Be aware that other people are a major source of disruption and the second disruptor is our technology, beeping constantly with text messages, social media postings, and non-critical email traffic.

Let's talk first about the people who really suck your time and energy from you. Don't let them derail your plans with their chatter, gossip or their pet peeve of the day. These individuals come in various personas, some of which I like to call the ramblers, the venters, and the gossips.

Ramblers are the people without focus. They waste time and don't get to the point. It's fine to listen to them for a bit because you have to respect that they are *trying* to convey something and may be thinking out loud. You don't want to prematurely shut down the creative process, but if it's unscheduled brainstorming and you don't have time to participate, try the following statement: "I can see you're still trying to sort through this problem. Why don't we book 15 minutes for tomorrow or the next day, once you've had a chance to collect your thoughts and put an action plan together? I'll have more time then to add to your brainstorming and try to give this some structure."

Then you have individuals who are the venters, the ones who just need to let off some steam, and want to use you as their personal therapist. If they feel comfortable enough to vent with you, then they consider you some kind of confidante, which means you can be frank with them. Try this: "I know this situation is frustrating you. And sometimes it's healthy to talk about the situation and get it out of your system. But if you dwell on it, it will consume you. I can already see that it's got you in a negative frame of mind, and it's probably time to move on. And if you ever feel yourself getting sucked into this kind of negative mindset, just drop me a text and I'll happily remind you how much stronger you are than this."

Different Types of Gossip

There will always be people in your workplace who want to gossip and talk about other people or pump you for information. Frivolous gossip does no good, and if you engage with the rumor mill, it will actually erode your credibility in addition to wasting your precious time. I like to shut down anyone who is gossiping immediately.

Sometimes it is *light gossip*, you know when someone is going on about cars, clothing, how much money people have, or who is dating who. Everyone engages in this kind of stuff at some point or other. In some situations, it can even be useful to understand connections or networks, but when it moves into the zone of irrelevant, petty, or dramatic, make every effort to rise above it. Try this: "I don't pay much attention to those types of things.

Everyone has different interests and goals in life. We need to respect those, and stay focused on the work and delivering results for the company." Another way to handle it is to say: "I'm sure *so and so* wouldn't want you telling me that. From what I've seen, they are trying to make a strong contribution here, and that's what matters."

But sometimes gossip can be deliberately harmful, and that can seriously impact someone's reputation. You may even find that this type of gossip can come from a group of co-workers who are seriously upset and spending too much time dwelling on what horrible thing a certain person has done.

I suggest that you deal with it this way: "I think everyone comes to work to be professional and do a good job. If you have a legitimate concern about someone's level of professionalism, then raise it with Human Resources or your manager. But if you're just hearing gossip, I recommend you don't repeat it. It's a serious thing to erode someone's reputation when you may not have all the facts."

Whenever I think about gossip and what a huge waste of time and energy it is, I am reminded of the words of social activist and First Lady Eleanor Roosevelt who said, "Great minds discuss ideas; average minds discuss events; small minds discuss people." *Don't become a small person.*

ESSENTIAL EXERCISE

CONTROL YOUR OWN DISTRACTING BEHAVIORS

Be aware that you could be your own worst enemy in terms of distractions. Face it, at some point, we all get in our own way. Here are some ideas and techniques that will help you deal with your own distractions.

- Your phone will distract you if you let it. Silence your phone when you are working on deadlines or attending meetings so you won't be constantly checking it for messages and calls. Phones are addictive. Remember, studies show that your brain releases the same kind of chemical when receiving a text message that addicts get when they get their fix.

- If you have a habit of procrastinating, fix it. *Period.* You probably have a whole list of habits that you do to make it look like you are busy, but the only reason you do them is so you can put off your actual daily assignments that are important. The techniques in this chapter regarding time management will help you overcome procrastination tendencies, and so can the tips within Chapter 8 about how to deliver results.

- You might be the rambler, the venter, or the gossip in your workplace and if so, it's time to stop those behaviors. Think about asking your peers for feedback about your habits and if there is anything you are doing – that you might not be aware of – that is wasting time. Let them know you are trying to improve upon your time management skills, and ask them to bring it to your attention the next time you might be wasting time rambling, venting, or gossiping. It will raise the whole team's level of awareness and change the dynamic in the group once everyone has "permission" to call out behaviors that are cutting into productivity.

Improving your Health and Wellness

There is no doubt about it, health and wellness are key success factors in how you will perform at work. The quality of your health is directly related to how productive you will be, how much energy you will have, and how clear your thinking is.

I encourage you to think about health and wellness in terms of mind, body, and spirit. I'll start with the mind and spend the most amount of time on that topic because we are in the midst of crisis in mental health. For just about any worker these days, there are way too many things to be stressed about, not the least being addictions or very bad habits they might be trying to overcome, struggles with self-confidence, school debt and financial worries, depression or anxiety, or having to be a primary caregiver to children and sometimes even older parents or grandparents at the same time.

When you think about it, your mind is the most powerful engine you have and when it's overwhelmed with worries, it can be totally exhausting. In the first chapter on attitude, we explored the power of "programming" your mind positively every day. Keeping your mind healthy with a positive mindset is one of the most effective ways to deal with work pressures and life stress.

The pressure today on just about every generation is enormous, even young people. In fact, studies show that a whopping 50% of Millennials are at high risk of depression, anxiety, or addiction. There are many reasons you can become overwhelmed with life. Here are just a few to consider which provide context for what you might be feeling.

- *You're always on, and you need a rest.* Downtime today is a rare thing. We are all tethered to our phones. There is little time to rest from the digital onslaught of information that is constantly seeking attention, in the form of likes, replies, and endless suggestions for ways to improve something about your appearance or intelligence.

- *You are very public, and need some privacy.* Every step you take or decision you make is in the spotlight, either because you put it there or because someone else thought it would be nice to share your information or image on their social platform. This has so many ripple effects in terms of additional interactions that pile up and which also need replies. Not only that, you may also feel constant nagging worries about what was shared by whom, why, and where.

- *You are redefining "success" and it's unclear and confusing.* Your parents mean well but when they tell you to get a job, get a degree, or buy a house, that can be challenging. It is the old standard of what "success" means, but today jobs aren't very plentiful, the pay often isn't enough to cover student debt, and homes are increasingly unaffordable. Perhaps you grew up in a nice home with a relatively well-off family and you want that for yourself, but you feel it's not attainable. So what does success look like for your generation? By its very nature, as you try to define this in your own terms, it's stressful.

• *You are putting off life decisions, and the constant comparisons are stressful.* What it is to be young is being redefined in our world and "young people" are now well into their mid to late 20s. Parental attention and support continues well into adulthood, and that is now the norm. Not surprisingly, more people are finding themselves closing in on age 30 and facing decisions that other generations grappled with when they were about 10 years younger than that. If you are caught up in these kinds of constant comparisons, you know how stressful it can be.

ESSENTIAL EXERCISE

OVERCOME OVERWHELM AND DAILY PRESSURES

With pressure mounting from so many aspects of modern life, it's a good idea to have some go-to coping mechanisms that you can call on when you get lonely, anxious, or completely overwhelmed. Here are some suggestions and techniques to help you on those darker days when you really feel a heavy weight on your shoulders.

- **Access EFAP Programs.** Explore the services provided by your employer's EFAP programs (stands for Employee and Family Assistance Programs). You'll be pleasantly surprised how much support is offered to help employees through major life moments.

- **Online Resources.** Look into online tools that can help you cope with anxieties you are facing. You can listen to guided meditations to relax your mind, or tap into experts who speak about how to break habits, think more positively, boost your self-confidence, or other practical lessons in life.

- **Self-help and Counseling.** Search out a self-help book or a counselor that addresses whatever issue you are grappling with, be it insomnia, addiction, finances, anxiety, caregiver's fatigue, OCD, or whatever. Fortunately any shame or stigma in seeking help is fading fast; the expectation today is that you can and should face any mental issues head-on and deal with them.

- **Put away the technology.** Do a digital detox once a week. Try going 24 hours without social media, gaming, TV, and other activity that you tend to overdo. Your brain will thank you for it because it actually needs time to process everything you've been feeding it. Opt instead for walking outside, meeting up with friends in person, doing some volunteer work, or trying a new hobby. Walking the dog and dancing are also great pursuits to refresh your mind.

- **Sleep when you need sleep.** You may feel pressured to be online or connected 24/7 in case you miss anything from work or from your social circles, but if this is causing you to miss sleep or get a very poor quality of sleep – that is something you need to resolve.

❖

ESSENTIAL EXERCISE

TAKE CARE OF YOUR PHYSICAL HEALTH

With all of the other pressures you are coping with, you really don't need your body to be another source of stress. Your body is a machine, and it will work for you or against you depending on how you treat it and take care of it.

Never before has there been more support and advice in society about ways to maintain physical health. But at the same time, society encourages us to overindulge in food, sodas, sweets, beer, and the latest treat on the market. This bombardment is all much too much, and our bodies are in a constant battle to try to stay well and operate properly.

Those of you who are healthy and treat your bodies well can skip right over this very brief section. Head on down to spirituality.

But for those of you who still tend to overindulge in poor food choices, empty calories, soft drinks, alcohol, tobacco, or recreational drugs, *what are you thinking?* We have access to so much information about healthy food choices, exercise, and prevention of disease that there's really no excuse not to take action when you should. See a doctor or therapist whenever you need to and follow their suggestions. Ignoring your physical body will hold you back from pursuing your dreams and getting ahead at work. That's just the way it is.

You know as well as I do that until you decide to take action, nothing will change. When you take good care of your body, you'll feel stronger, smarter, more energetic, and better able to take on your goals. Here are the basic three steps.

1 *Eat well.* Educate yourself about what you are eating and what it is doing to your body. Make changes where needed.

2 *Get enough exercise.* If your job is sedentary, get up and walk around at least once every hour. Walk to work. Find a gym near your work. Go.

3 *Sleep.* Get a sufficient amount of good quality sleep each night so your body can repair itself.

Spirituality in Our Modern World

In our survey, just 18% of Millennials say they take time daily for a spiritual practice that keeps them centered and connected to something bigger. Most of these people say they wish they had more time for a spiritual practice because it would really improve their lives and help them find meaning in their life.

These findings echo academic studies that are showing that Millennials tend to be less religious than previous generations, and yet some of them still say that they value spirituality, prayer, and meditation. They seem to know spirituality can help them live a more peaceful and calm life, and stay relaxed and happy.

Nonetheless, most Millennials remain unclear about their thoughts in terms of spirituality and can benefit from help understanding what it is all about.

Just before ending this brief section, I want to share a few points to ponder if you are contemplating or redefining your own beliefs.

- Spirituality is a very broad concept that every human explores at some point. Most of us face it when we are grappling with hard times, the loss of a loved one, or some kind of sudden tragic news.
- Be open minded about your time here on earth and how you are connected to others.
- Be curious about traditions and experiment with new things like yoga, meditation, and prayer. Billions of people around the world can't be completely wrong about the power of spirit.
- Own your journey. How you choose to identify with your spirit is for you to decide. What I can tell you for sure is that you have inside you the capacity to catapult your clarity, purpose, and happiness in life. *We all do.*

ESSENTIAL EXERCISE

TAKE STOCK OF YOUR HEALTH AND TAKE STEPS TO IMPROVE IT

If you want to achieve overall balance in your life, it's time to take care of your mind, body, and spirit in equal measure. Use the following questions as a jumping-off point to assess how you are feeling right now about your health and your overall spiritual outlook on life.

Be specific in your answers and then think of some concrete ways you could start to improve upon the way you are feeling to enjoy more consistent health and peace in your life.

- How do you describe your mental health? Are there actions you could be taking right now to become stronger and healthier? If needed, set out some specific initial actions and timelines so you can begin to create a better mental health outlook.

- How do you describe your physical health? Are there actions you could be taking right now to become stronger and healthier? Do you need to become more active? If so, choose something fun because you'll be more likely to stick with it. Set some specific initial action steps and timelines that will allow you to achieve better overall physical health.

- How do you describe your spiritual health? Are there actions you could be taking right now to develop or improve your spiritual outlook on life? Set some specific initial actions and timelines so you can reach a place of greater peace and serenity in your life.

KEY POINTS FROM CHAPTER 10

- Be aware of all your personal needs: mental, physical, and spiritual.
- We all have different energy levels, stress points, sleep needs, and recharge techniques. Understand yours.
- Learn and practice ways to minimize distractions because the higher you rise within the workplace, the more distractions there will be.
- Be aware of people around you who drag you down and deplete your energy.
- Procrastination is your enemy. Catch yourself when it happens and practice ways to overcome it.
- Become really clear on what is needed and by when.
- Create false deadlines (early deadlines) for you and your team so stress is minimized.
- Take responsibility for the quality and direction of your own life.
- Consider exploring spirituality and mindfulness to bring more peace and joy into your life.

AFTERWORD

The idea behind the *10 Essentials® for the Motivated Millennial* was to pass along career advice to help you and the next generation of leaders to rise up more quickly, to give you a head-start so you can claim your rightful place. *Why?*

Quite simply, the world urgently needs you. It needs you to be successful, to realize all of your potential, and to perform at your best. Older generations are retiring. Existing work cultures need a breath of fresh air. The world needs your global mindset and will benefit from your thirst for learning and growth.

Within the new world of work, your collaborative approach is invaluable because you understand that diversity makes teams and decisions much stronger. Furthermore, you have proven yourself fearless in your adoption of technology, your quest for productivity, and your desire to make a positive difference in the world.

In working through the *10 Essentials*®, you've gained dozens of proven strategies to help you perform even better at work and to live your best life. I envy you the opportunity to shape a new definition of success in this world, and I wish you happiness and peace as you pursue your dreams.

– Robyn

CHECKLIST OF
ESSENTIAL EXERCISES

ACKNOWLEDGMENTS

I've always dreamed of writing a book to inspire the next generation. I wrote it down as a goal years ago in one of my very first annual life plans. I wasn't sure how that would manifest itself, but I knew that I wanted to pay it forward.

I knew this so early because I was blessed with amazing mentors who always set the example of building the next generation of talent. They believed in me, invested in me, challenged me, and nurtured my talents. If you meet a leader of this caliber in your lifetime, you will be extremely fortunate. I have had many and to them, I am forever grateful: Linda Forestell, Gerry Pond, Bob Neal, and Steve Palmer. You opened doors when I was just starting out and continue to inspire me today.

To Jay Forbes, Lynn Joliffe, Keith Bradley, Paul Bay and Alain Maquet: You challenged me to move out of my comfort zone, go global, and realize more of my potential. You trusted me and sent me into unknown territory, time and time again, with the full confidence I would succeed. I am a better person and leader because you encouraged me.

Thanks also goes to the exceptional trainers I've had. Brent Finnamore and Wayne Harrison: You both helped me in my very early career days and shaped much of my thinking around personal performance. Kelly Langille and Marg Taylor: Your guidance and full support of our dreams has been the true definition of partnership. And to Kathryn Bishop and Gayle Peterson, thank you for including me in your first-ever pioneering program for Women Transforming Leadership at Oxford, and for fostering such an incredible network of passionate leaders around the globe. Amanda Poole, you showed up in my life at the right time with the right guidance, and life has never been the same.

Thanks goes to Simone Graham whose enthusiasm for this project was evident from our first chance meeting one summer night in Grand Digue, New Brunswick. I am most grateful to have such an experienced and world renowned editor bring her crispness and clarity to my ideas.

And to Janice Brown who always seems to blend creativity and class – thank you. Your graphic designs capture the essence of what I am trying to say, and I am blessed to have such a trusted collaborator on so many projects that mean so much to me.

Above all, I want to thank my family. To my husband Brent: Words cannot express how much I appreciate your unwavering support of every single dream I dream. To our beautiful daughters Olivia Ann-Marie and Mary Grace: You inspire me every day to be a better person and to make the world a better place. To Mom and Dad: I couldn't have asked for better role models and champions. To my sisters and their wonderful families, and of course to my in-laws: Thank you all for your constant support and encouragement.

ABOUT THE AUTHOR

Robyn Tingley is a sought-after speaker and trainer who has presented to audiences worldwide, and specializes in advice for women and Millennials – two groups, that together, account for more than half of today's workforce and growing.

Robyn has lived and worked around the world as a corporate executive for a Fortune 100 company with responsibilities spanning four continents. She launched three social enterprises by the age of 40, and advises blue chips, start-ups, and Canada's most entrepreneurial university, UNB. She created the *10 Essentials*® books and workshops to provide practical modern-day career advice which is based on her first-hand knowledge of corporate culture, entrepreneurial ventures, life experience, and leadership success.

Robyn was named to the *Women Worth Watching* list of top female executive trailblazers in Europe and North America and she was selected as one of the *Most Powerful & Influential Women in California*. She was honored to be chosen as one of 30 women worldwide for Oxford University's Inaugural Women Transforming Leadership program.

Robyn is both a citizen of the world and a proud Canadian. She lives now in her home province of New Brunswick with her husband and two young daughters.

www.RobynTingley.com

76826307R00125

Made in the USA
Columbia, SC
17 September 2017